Development Centre Studies

Youth Aspirations and the Reality of Jobs in Developing Countries

MIND THE GAP

This work is published under the responsibility of the Secretary-General of the OECD. The opinions expressed and arguments employed herein do not necessarily reflect the official views of the member countries of the OECD or its Development Centre.

This document, as well as any data and any map included herein, are without prejudice to the status of or sovereignty over any territory, to the delimitation of international frontiers and boundaries and to the name of any territory, city or area.

Please cite this publication as:
OECD (2017), *Youth Aspirations and the Reality of Jobs in Developing Countries: Mind the Gap*, Development Centre Studies, OECD Publishing, Paris.
http://dx.doi.org/10.1787/9789264285668-en

ISBN 978-92-64-28565-1 (print)
ISBN 978-92-64-28566-8 (PDF)

Series: Development Centre Studies
ISSN 1563-4302 (print)
ISSN 1990-0295 (online)

The statistical data for Israel are supplied by and under the responsibility of the relevant Israeli authorities. The use of such data by the OECD is without prejudice to the status of the Golan Heights, East Jerusalem and Israeli settlements in the West Bank under the terms of international law.

Photo credits: Cover © design by the OECD Development Centre

Foreword

What would young people like to do when they grow up? Will they be able to fulfil their job aspirations? Will they be attracted by sectors that have potential for sustainable development and secure livelihoods? More than ever before, we need to better understand the employment preferences of young men and women in the developing world. Digging into youth aspirations is incredibly important if we are to harness the tremendous energy and talent of young people, make potential growth sectors more attractive to them, and ultimately contain the chilling effects that unmet youth aspirations can have on society.

This study places youth employment preferences at the forefront of the analysis. It argues that young people are well-off to the extent that their employment preferences are satisfied. It then goes on to investigate the extent to which the aspirations of young people are aligned with the reality of jobs in the developing world. A key message of this study is that existing jobs in developing countries do not live up to youth aspirations and that policy makers and development partners should take this reality more seriously. Reducing the youth employment preferences gap will take time, but it is possible. National policy makers should focus on a two-pronged strategy to address the misalignment in youth job aspirations and the availability of realistic employment opportunities. First, they need to help young people shape career aspirations that are realistic and that can fit with the world they will be entering. Second, they need to improve the quality of jobs vis-à-vis those job conditions that matter for young people.

This study therefore adds to the debate on youth employment in three important ways. First, it constitutes an unprecedented effort to analyse the nature and the determinants of youth employment preferences in a wide range of developing countries that are socially, economically and politically diverse . Second, it provides unique empirical evidence on the gap between youth aspirations and the reality of jobs. Third, it proposes policy directions to help address the youth employment preference gap in developing countries.

This report contributes to the work of the OECD Development Centre on building more cohesive societies and helping countries identify emerging issues and find innovative solutions to address social challenges. It was undertaken as part of the Youth Inclusion project, co-funded by the European Union and implemented by the OECD Development Centre, to analyse policies for youth and provide evidence for the policy dialogue on youth well-being in developing and emerging countries. It is based on the harmonisation and analysis of data from 32 developing countries in Africa, Asia, Europe and Latin America.

We believe this study is a source of information for decision makers in charge of education and employment policies across developing countries. We hope they apply the findings to meet the rising aspirations of young people in the world of work and reach the ambitious target of decent work for all captured in Sustainable Development Goal 8.

Mario Pezzini
Director of the Development Centre
and Special Advisor to the OECD Secretary-General on Development

Acknowledgements

The report was prepared by the Social Cohesion Unit of the OECD Development Centre as part of the Youth Inclusion project.

The team was led by Alexandre Kolev, Head of the Social Cohesion Unit, and Ji-Yeun Rim, Co-ordinator of the Youth Inclusion project, under the guidance of Mario Pezzini, Director of the OECD Development Centre and Special Advisor to the OECD Secretary-General on Development, and Naoko Ueda, Deputy-Director of the OECD Development Centre. The report was drafted by Alexandre Kolev and Adrien Lorenceau, with the help of Norbert Rugambage for the statitical and exploratory analysis and with research assistance provided by Jonathan Broekhuizen and Manas Pathak.

The authors are grateful to Sara Elder for her valuable input, help and interest in this project as well as for her invitation to participate to the Work4Youth 2016 Global Symposium in Geneva. Together with Sara Elder, the Work4Youth team at the International Labour Office (ILO), and especially Marco Minocri, Marco Principi and Marcelo Segovia, provided precious help and guidance in accessing and comprehending the School to Work Transition Survey data, which are at the center of this analysis.

The report benefited from the insightful comments of Rohen d'Aiglepierre (Agence Française de Développement, AFD), Céline Gradatour (AFD), Kiril Kiryakov (European Union, EU), Mattias Lundberg (World Bank), and Maria Rosa de Paolis (EU). It was reviewed by OECD colleagues Romina Boarini (General Secretariat, SGE), Marco Mira d'Ercole (Statistics Directorate, STD), Sebastian Königs (Employment, Labour and Social Affairs, ELS), Sam Mealy (SGE), Fabrice Murtin (STD). It also benefited from valuable input and comments from Marcus Böhme (Development Centre), Ian Brand-Weiner (Development Centre), Bram Dekker (Development Centre), Sarah Kups (Development Centre), Hyeshin Park (Development Centre), Ji-Yeun Rim (Development Centre), and Pablo Suárez-Robles (Development Centre).

Mary Bortin edited the manuscript and Delphine Grandrieux oversaw production of the publication.

The Youth Inclusion project is co-financed by the European Union.

Table of contents

Tables

Abbreviations and acronyms

FYROM	Former Yugoslav Republic of Macedonia
ICT	Information and Communication Technology
ILO	International Labour Organization
ISCO	International Standard Classification of Occupations
ISIC	International Standard Industry Classification
LAC	Latin America and the Caribbean
NGO	Non-governmental organisation
OECD	Organisation for Economic Co-operation and Development
SWTS	School to Work Transition Survey
UN	United Nations

Many governments in developing countries are realising that the quality of jobs matters for development and that dedicated efforts are needed to support the transition from school to decent work. However, little is known on what actually matters for young people in terms of job characteristics and employment conditions, and to what extent youth aspirations can fit with the world they will be entering. Answering these questions is important for a diverse audience of policy makers seeking to enhance youth well-being, raise labour productivity and contain the chilling effects that unmet youth aspirations can generate on society.

The main objective of this study is to inform decision makers on the need to act on the broad misalignment between youth employment preferences and the reality of labour market. It prompts the following key questions: What is the nature of youth career aspirations and job-related drivers of job satisfaction? What shapes such employment preferences? How likely is it that young people will be able to meet their job aspirations? What can policy makers do to reduce the gap between youth preferences and the reality of jobs?

The study is based on the harmonisation and analysis of data from 32 school-to-work transition surveys (SWTS) conducted by the International Labour Organization (ILO) in developing and transition countries in Africa, Asia, Europe and Latin America and the Caribbean (LAC). This study adds to the global debate on youth employment and job quality in three important ways.

First, it provides for the first time ever a detailed comparative analysis of two critical components of youth employment preferences across the developing world: i) career aspirations of young people aged 15 to 29 who are enrolled at any education level, and ii) job facets that raise job satisfaction based on workers aged 15 to 29. The study shows that young people in developing countries enter the labour market with high career aspirations. In many developing countries and at all education levels, most students aspire to work for the public sector and in highly skilled professions. By and large, youth career aspirations are driven by the social position of young people in society, with the notable exception of female students, who have high career preferences regardless of their background. Using an adjusted measure of job satisfaction that includes information on the desire to change jobs, this study further indicates that a number of job characteristics are associated with greater job satisfaction. Important drivers of job satisfaction in all countries include being self-employed by choice or because it is required by the family, the skill intensity of jobs, having the right skills for the job, training opportunities, job security, formality and labour earnings.

Second, the study assesses the extent to which youth aspirations are aligned with real job characteristics and employment conditions. It shows that, in many developing and emerging countries, existing jobs do not live up to youth aspirations. On the one hand, career aspirations of young people have little in common with current and projected labour demand. Career aspiration gaps are found to be broad everywhere, but their depth differs across world regions. The challenge of unrealistic career aspirations is greatest in Africa and LAC. A major concern is that the gap between youth career aspirations and the reality of the labour market persists for tertiary-educated youth. On the other hand, several employment and job characteristics that make young workers unhappy – such as low-skilled and agriculture employment, job insecurity, informality, skills mismatch and the lack of training opportunities – are relatively common in developing countries.

Third, the study suggests priority areas for policy makers. To address the misalignment between youth employment preferences and the availability of realistic employment opportunities, the report argues, national policy makers should focus on a two-pronged strategy of: i) helping young people shape career aspirations based on relevant labour market information so that they do not build unrealistic expectations, and ii) improving the quality of jobs with due regard to those job conditions that matter for young people. To be realistic, this strategy would also need to be tailored to specific country contexts and recognise that the process of narrowing the gap between youth employment preferences and the reality of jobs may take time. This strategy could be articulated around the following eight goals:

- Guide student learning and career choices.
- Unlock youth entrepreneurship potential.
- Make agriculture and medium-skilled occupations more attractive.
- Extend social protection to workers in the non-state sector.
- Address job security concerns.
- Make work pay.
- Reduce skills mismatch.
- Support formal labour relations.

Policy makers across the world are preoccupied with the great challenge of helping millions of young people find decent work, as conveyed in Goal 8 of the 2030 Agenda for Sustainable Development. The challenge is particularly daunting in developing countries where, in the face of large informal labour markets and weak enforcement of labour standards, many young people are obliged to take low-quality jobs for their very survival and end up as the working poor. This has led many governments in developing countries to realise that good jobs matter for development and that dedicated efforts are needed to boost the quality of jobs and make work pay. It is striking, however, how little attention has been paid so far to exploring what actually matters for young people in terms of job characteristics and employment conditions. Today, in many developing and emerging countries, a key development challenge is that existing jobs do not live up to youth aspirations.

This study takes an alternative route in revisiting youth labour-market performance and the quality of jobs in developing countries. It places youth employment preferences at the forefront of the analysis and asks: What is the nature of youth career aspirations and job-related drivers of job satisfaction? What shapes such employment preferences? How likely is it that young people will be able to meet their job aspirations? What can policy makers do to reduce the gap between youth preferences and the reality of jobs?

Answering these questions is important for a diverse audience of policy makers seeking to enhance youth well-being, raise labour productivity and contain the chilling effects that unmet youth aspirations can generate on society. If youth employment preferences mirror the reality of jobs and can be satisfied, youth may indeed enjoy well-being. Young people who can fulfil their career aspirations and find jobs that bring about greater satisfaction at work are also likely to be more productive in the workplace and in society at large. In contrast, failing to shape such preferences in the light of the reality of the world of work can have serious economic, social and political consequences. Unmet career aspirations and job dissatisfaction can contribute to low productivity, low motivation, absenteeism, accidents, health problems and a lower level of life satisfaction. It is also often argued that difficulty in fulfilling aspirations in the world of work can be a precursor to other issues and problems in society, including social unrest and large migration outflows.

An important objective of this study is to inform decision makers on the need to act on the large youth job aspiration gap. The study involved harmonisation and analysis of data from school-to-work transition surveys (SWTS) collected between 2012 and 2015 in 32 developing and transition countries in Africa, Asia, Europe and Latin America and Caribbean (LAC).[1] It outlines a number of common trends as well as regional and country specificities. An attempt is made to identify some of the most important issues and to suggest priority areas for policy makers. In doing so, the study also echoes broader concerns on the need to give more weight and consideration to people's well-being in the measurement of social and economic development.

Insights into youth career aspirations

At all education levels, young people in developing countries enter the labour market with high career aspirations. Insights on youth career aspirations are derived from information gathered in 32 developing countries from students aged 15 to 29 about the sector of activity and the type of jobs they would like to hold later in life. In many developing countries and at all education levels, most students prefer to work for the public sector. The share of students who want to work in the public sector is particularly high in Africa, where it ranges from 65% in Tanzania to 78% in Zambia. Becoming self-employed or working for a private company appear to be more attractive to students in more advanced economies, particularly in Latin America where around a third of students say they are ready to work in each of these sectors. Data on occupational preferences further show that most students in the 32 countries examined – 80% on average – aspire to work in high-skilled occupations, at levels 1 to 3 of the International Standard Classification of Occupations (ISCO). Conversely, few students want to work in intermediate-skilled occupations (ISCO 4-8).

By and large, youth career aspirations are driven by young people's position in society, with the notable exception of female students, who have high career preferences. Youth career aspirations are influenced by factors that affect the way one perceives oneself, commonly referred to as self-concept factors. These factors often relate to demographic or family characteristics, socio-economic status and academic performance. Overall, high career expectations mirror the fact that, in developing countries today, many young people are more educated than their parents. Other characteristics matter as well. Disadvantaged students tend to have high employment preferences for the public sector and little attraction for self-employment, and students from rural areas or low-income households are attracted by less-skilled occupations. Moreover, as young people shape their goals about the future, their parents' jobs tend to influence their decisions. Indeed, students' occupational preferences and their fathers' occupations are closely correlated. There is also a strong gender dimension in career aspirations, as the fact of being a woman increases a person's preference for the public sector and high-skilled occupations, and reduces the desire to become self-employed.

Job facets that influence job satisfaction

Facets of job satisfaction add to the understanding of job quality. Traditional approaches to the measurement of job quality rely on objective indicators that influence well-being. Evidence, mostly from member countries of the Organisation for Economic Co-operation and Development (OECD), highlights the importance of several job characteristics on people's well-being, such as earnings, benefits and job security. Uncovering the link between employment characteristics and job satisfaction can further enrich the policy dialogue on job quality from a subjective well-being perspective. This is very much needed in low- and middle-income countries, where the knowledge gap on those issues is wider. There are inherent advantages in relying on job satisfaction measures to document job quality and employment preferences, but there are also limitations that necessitate careful interpretation of the findings. However, assuming that well-being is sufficiently correlated with preference satisfaction, it is reasonable to believe that young people who are satisfied with their jobs will be better off.

Facets of job satisfaction are derived from an adjusted measure of job satisfaction

In this study, facets of job satisfaction are derived from statistical correlation between an adjusted and more restrictive measure of job satisfaction and a set of employment characteristics, controlling for other socio-demographic factors. Measurement consistency is improved by using a restrictive measure of job satisfaction that combines a generic measure of job satisfaction on a Likert scale with information about people's desire to change jobs. Indeed, about 28% of youth declare themselves satisfied with their current employment situation but still want to change jobs to find better or more secure employment, and are thus considered in this study as not really satisfied. As a result, with a more restrictive definition of job satisfaction, around half of young workers (49%) are considered truly satisfied with their jobs, compared to 77% of young workers with the more relaxed definition. Satisfaction displays heterogeneity across countries in terms of the share of satisfied workers who do not want to change jobs, ranging from 17% in Zambia to 77% in Moldova.

A number of job characteristics are associated with greater job satisfaction. Employment status is one characteristic that seems to matter a great deal. Compared to wage employment, self-employment is associated with a higher level of job satisfaction among young workers across nearly all the 32 countries under consideration, but only when it is by choice or required by the family, and not by default in the absence of wage employment opportunities. The association between job satisfaction and self-employment is particularly high for female workers. The analysis also provides insights into the interplay between the skill intensity of jobs and job satisfaction. Low-skilled occupations correlate with a lower level of job satisfaction in all countries. This is also true of medium-skilled occupations, but only in countries in transition and Latin American countries. The analysis further highlights the importance of having the right skills for the job. Skills mismatch – whether measured as over or under qualification in either education or skills – turns out to be a strong driver of dissatisfaction at work, particularly when individuals are overqualified. The evidence further indicates that some activities, such as agriculture, provide a low level of job satisfaction among young people. Moreover, in nearly all countries, job security, formality and labour earnings stand out clearly as important drivers of job satisfaction. Income levels and being offered training appear to contribute more to satisfaction in urban areas, while informality is particularly detrimental to job satisfaction among female and rural young workers.

From youth employment preferences to reality

A key challenge for most developing and emerging countries is ensuring that idealistic career aspirations do not transform into unrealistic expectations on the labour market. When career aspirations affect young people's educational choices, the alignment between youth career aspirations and the reality of the labour market becomes critical to understanding youth well-being, productivity and youth labour-market performance. Evidence from SWTS and the ILO's employment projections indicate that youth career aspirations by skills level are overly optimistic in the light of today's and tomorrow's labour-market needs. Overall, about 60% of students wishing to work in highly skilled occupation will be unlikely fulfil their career aspirations, while as many as 73% of young workers who occupy a medium-skilled job, and 80% who occupy a low-skilled job, may be unable to satisfy their career preferences. Using employment projections for the coming years yields similar results and points to a large misalignment in youth career preferences by level of skills and projected labour demand. What is remarkable is that career aspiration gaps by skills level are broad everywhere, but the depth differs across world regions and is particularly pronounced in Africa and Latin America. Strong youth employment preferences for the public sector, observed in all regions of the developing world, are also unlikely to be satisfied. On average across countries, as many as 40% of students wishing to work for the public sector are unlikely to find a wage job in that sector.

A major concern is that the gap between youth career aspirations and the reality of the labour market persists for tertiary-educated youth. On average across the 32 countries, around 48% of tertiary-educated individuals wishing to work legitimately in a highly skilled job will likely be unable to do so. While career aspirations of students in tertiary education are similar across countries, the mismatch with the reality of jobs is less pronounced in more developed economies where employment opportunities for the highly skilled are greater. Africa stands out as the region with the largest share of tertiary educated workers engaged in medium- or low-skilled jobs. Remarkably, students' career aspirations do not always reflect earning differentials across occupations. In countries like Armenia, Benin, Kyrgyzstan, Lebanon, Liberia, Peru, Tanzania and Ukraine, and in territories like West Bank and Gaza Strip, average earnings are higher for medium-skilled and/or low-skilled occupations than for high-skilled occupations, and thus cannot explain the large misalignment in career aspirations and the reality of jobs.

Another key challenge is the gap between facets of job satisfaction and the reality of job conditions. Improving job quality in areas that matter the most for young people can not only lead to greater economic benefits but can also enhance youth well-being. Two types of insights emerge from confronting facets of job satisfaction with real employment conditions. On the positive side, a number of facets that raise job satisfaction, such as being self-employed by choice or as required by the family, tend to be observed among a non-negligible proportion of young people in low-income countries. In the Republic of the Congo (Congo) and Malawi, one out of three young workers is self-employed by choice. On the less positive side, a number of employment characteristics and job conditions that drive down job satisfaction are relatively common in developing countries. This is the case for low-skilled employment, which constitutes a quarter or more of youth employment in Brazil, El Salvador, Peru, Tanzania, Viet Nam, West Bank and Gaza Strip, and Zambia, or for agriculture, which is the main source of jobs for more than 40% of young workers in Kyrgyzstan, Madagascar, Nepal and Togo. It is also true for other job facets that make young workers unhappy, such as low job security, informality, skills mismatch and lack of training opportunities. Job insecurity is particularly pronounced in countries such as Egypt, Malawi, Montenegro, Peru and Viet Nam, where 50% or more of all young wage employees work as temporary employees with fixed-term employment contracts. Informality is dominant in Africa, where it concerns 80% of young workers, and widespread in Asia and Latin America, where respectively 48% and 33% of youth workers are in a non-registered activity. As regards skills mismatch, it concerns 55% of young workers, and only a small number of them (20% on average) are offered training opportunities.

Closing the gap on youth employment preferences

There is an urgent need to act now on the large gap between youth aspirations and the reality of the labour markets. Matching youth career aspirations and facets of job satisfaction with the reality of labour markets can play an essential role in youth well-being and social cohesion in general. Yet the evidence for the 32 developing countries examined in this study indicates that the career aspirations of young people have little in common with current and projected labour demand, and that several job characteristics that young people value and that raise their satisfaction at work are pretty rare in many of these countries. There is good reason to believe that it is a significant problem. Misalignment in youth employment preferences and the availability of realistic employment prospects makes it much less likely that young people will experience smooth school-to-work transitions. A large gap might decrease motivation and productivity, fuel frustration, hamper well-being and even result in social unrest.

Reducing the youth employment preferences gap will take time, but it is possible. To address the misalignment in youth employment preferences and the availability of realistic employment opportunities, national policy makers should focus on a two-pronged strategy of: i) helping young people shape career aspirations that are realistic and that can fit with the world they will be entering, and ii) improving the quality of jobs with due regard to the job conditions that matter for young people. To be realistic, this strategy would need to be tailored to specific country contexts and to recognise that the process of narrowing the gap between youth preferences and reality may take time.

An effective approach requires a policy package consisting of short-term and long-term goals. This strategy could be articulated around the following eight goals: 1) guide student learning and career choices; 2) unlock youth entrepreneurship potential; 3) make agriculture more attractive; 4) extend social protection to workers in the non-state sector; 5) address job security concerns; 6) make work pay; 7) reduce skills mismatches; and 8) support more formal labour relations.

1. **Guide student learning and career choices.** While it is important that young people do not give up on their dreams or curtail their ambitions, policy makers need to ensure that young people can access accurate information about labour market prospects and effective guidance on the best way to get closer to their goals. Better and well-informed career guidance and counselling is thus necessary. This requires the development of sound education and labour market information systems so that relevant and regular information about education outcomes and employment opportunities can be collected and analysed. Education and training providers have a key role to play both in the provision of adequate counselling and by taking account of youth aspirations in programme development. The spread of information and communication technology (ICT) among young people in developing countries can also offer innovative ways to reach out, help them make important decisions about their future, learn about education pathways, employment opportunities and skills needs, adapt their ideas about careers and make smart decisions when choosing subjects to study and seeking work experience.

2. **Unlock youth entrepreneurship potential.** While self-employment stands out as a key driver of job satisfaction when it is by choice or required by the family, it is important to recognise that, in many developing countries, only a tiny number of young entrepreneurs with specific characteristics prove to be successful and the majority end up in subsistence activities. A comprehensive approach is needed to address the diversity of enabling and disabling factors to higher entrepreneurial performance, and this includes well-designed entrepreneurship promotion programmes. Recent evidence makes a strong case for redirecting entrepreneurship programmes towards young people with the highest entrepreneurship potential and refocusing such programmes on business development services and on a package of training and access to finance services that have proven to work best for micro-entrepreneurs.

3. **Make agriculture and medium-skilled occupations more attractive.** Agriculture is currently a major employer in many developing countries and the sector has the space to create more jobs for youth, both as entrepreneurs and wage workers in agriculture and food processing. In many developing countries, the challenge is to raise job satisfaction in agriculture, where the jobs are tough and the pay is low. Making agriculture more attractive for youth calls for interventions on many fronts. Employment in the agriculture sector must first be transformed into decent jobs to attract youth, starting with better incomes for farmers and the modernisation of agriculture practices that address environmental concerns. Rural and market infrastructures need to be improved with a view to improving access to education, training, inputs, markets, technology (including ICT) and finance. Based on the needs of local and national markets and consumers, policies and programmes can support the strengthening of smallholders and small and medium-sized agro businesses and create specific incentives for youth, for example by supporting youth co-operatives and providing financial and/or technical support to businesses that hire young people. Directing investments to secondary towns can create new markets for commercial family farming/local productions, contributing to the creation of farm and off-farm employment for youth in rural and semi-rural areas. Moreover, supporting the diffusion of new technologies and digitalisation, notably across medium-skilled occupations, can help increase the attractiveness of new jobs that otherwise would not be very popular among youth.

4. **Extend social protection to workers in the non-state sector**. In many developing countries, social security provision remains largely biased towards state-sector workers. As a result, public employment is largely preferred by young people, in particular women and vulnerable workers. Creating a modern non-state sector that can be attractive for youth cannot be achieved without the development of comprehensive national social protection systems that will extend coverage to formal private sector workers and, gradually, to informal workers.

5. **Address job security concerns**. While job security is an important driver of job satisfaction, a large number of young people are unlikely to find stable employment. Offering greater job security through more stable contractual arrangements in the wage sector is important not only for improving improve youth well-being at work, but also in order to help firms attract suitably skilled workers and to provide incentives for investing in skills development. There is also a need to protect workers against income loss. In countries that lack unemployment benefits, employment protection provisions such as severance pay can sustain dismissed workers as they search for new jobs and improve job matching, but these provisions need better enforcement.

6. **Make work pay**. As part of a broader agenda to improve job quality in developing countries, dedicated efforts are needed to raise the labour productivity and earning capacity of low-paid workers. This means that governments should continue to invest in the quality of education for all and enshrine equal pay for women and men in the law. There is also a need to reconnect labour productivity gains with changes in wages and to ensure that companies and the people who own and run them are able to pass along the benefits and lift the living standards of workers. In countries where unions are weak and not able to prevent low wages in the productive sector, minimum wage policy can be an effective way to protect low wage earners – including informal workers, who can use minimum wages as a benchmark to negotiate their salaries. Sound policy design is necessary to establish the correct minimum wage level, however. Minimum wages that are too low or too high in relation to the median wage and other local economic parameters are unlikely to address the problem of low-paid work. To be meaningful, minimum wages also need to cover a broad range of workers and must be enforced by a credible mechanism.

7. **Reduce skills mismatch**. Better management of youth skills can lead to economic benefits and increase the well-being of young workers. A package of measures to reduce the skills mismatch includes providing high-quality career guidance counselling to young people, investing in the quality, relevance and responsiveness of education and initial training, and developing opportunities to learn on the job and to receive continuing training at work. Moreover, overall skills development and matching policies should be seen as an integral part of a broader development strategy and should address specific country constraints. In many low-income countries, policy makers need to provide the right incentives to small and medium-sized enterprises (SMEs) for training young people. They also need to identify delivery modalities that work in the context of high informality and that respond to the large number of out-of-school youth without basic skills (functional literacy and numeracy).

8. **Support more formal labour relations**. While it is unlikely that most young informal producers and workers can be formalised in the short term, efforts should be made. To this end, an important medium-term policy objective is to decrease the costs and increase the benefits of working formally. For youth entrepreneurs, the benefits of operating formally often relate to the possibility of enjoying the legal ownership of their place of business and means of production, benefitting from

enforceable commercial contracts and tax breaks, or being covered by affordable social protection schemes. The costs of entry into the formal economy include the need to pay taxes and social security contributions, obtain a license or register their accounts. The cost-benefit ratio may be different for informal wage workers, for whom formalisation mostly means obtaining a formal wage job with a secure contract and statutory social protection.

Note

1. Throughout the report, countries in transition is based on the United Nations country classification used in the World Economic Situation and Prospects 2014 report (available here: www.un.org/en/development/desa/policy/wesp/wesp_current/wesp2014.pdf) and refer to former Armenia, Kyrgyzstan, Former Yugoslav Republic of Macedonia (FYROM), Moldova, Montenegro, Russian Federation, Serbia and Ukraine.

Chapter 1

Insights into youth career aspirations in developing countries

"What would you like to do when you grow up?" is a simple, commonly asked question. Whether or not youth career aspirations are fulfilled can provide insights into youth well-being. This chapter places youth employment preferences at the forefront and asks two crucial questions: What is the nature of youth career aspirations? And what shapes such preferences? The chapter begins by exploring in detail the sectors of activity and types of occupations that appeal to students aged 15-29 in 32 developing countries. It then investigates how various socio-economic characteristics of young people may shape such aspirations.

Career aspirations constitute an important driver of individuals' life paths and can play an essential role in well-being if they can be fulfilled. While high career aspirations can motivate individuals to thrive in life and society, setting unrealistic objectives might decrease motivation and fuel deception, resulting in lower productivity at work and lesser well-being. Career aspirations are of particular importance for young people as they make important decisions about their future at secondary school, notably in terms of choosing which studies to pursue. Such decisions are critical for the ultimate labour market prospects of young people.

Youth career aspirations are understood in this report as students' career preferences. Insights are derived from information gathered from students aged 15 to 29 in 32 developing countries about the sector of activity and type of job they would like to occupy later in life (see Box 1.1 for more details about the School-to-Work Transition Surveys, SWTS). More precisely, students were asked: "Ideally, who would you like to work for?" and "Ideally, what type of work would you like to do?" They were asked to select both an ideal sector of activity (among the choices presented in Figure 1.1) and an ideal occupation (Figure 1.2). In this sense, the analysis focuses on the idealistic component of career aspirations (career preferences), and not on the realistic component (career expectation). Career preferences are likely to affect students' educational choices and thus to impact their labour market outcome and job satisfaction later on (AfDB/OECD/UNDP/UNECA, 2012).

Young people enter the labour market with high career aspirations

In many countries, especially in Africa, a large number of students would like to work in the public sector. The share of students wishing to work in the public sector, including international organisations and non-governmental organisations (NGOs), is particularly high in Africa, where it ranges from 65% in Tanzania to 78% in Zambia (Figure 1.1). In contrast, the public sector appeals to only around a third of youth Latin America and the Caribbean (LAC) on average – but the region displays large heterogeneity, with 26% of Brazilian students interested by the public sector compared to 45% in Jamaica. Interestingly, the public sector remains an attractive perspective in transition countries, possibly due to the historical importance of the public sector in these countries. Overall, this result confirms that public employment remains substantially valued by young people in many developing countries, most likely because it often combines characteristics that are valued by young workers such as job formality, stability or security. This preference might also influence the way young men and women make decisions about subjects chosen and experience sought.

The private sector seems more attractive for students in richer economies. Self-employment (or family business) and private companies appeal to more young people in more advanced economies in general. This is particularly the case in LAC, where around a third of students say they are tempted to work in each of these sectors. The figures probably mirror the greater opportunities that are available in this segment of the labour market. In Peru for example, 54% of students would like to work in a private company. In Colombia and El Salvador, respectively 36% and 46% of students are interested in joining a private company, but the data cover urban areas only.

Most students would like to work in top-skilled occupations. When students are asked which type of occupation they would like to occupy, the vast majority declare that they would like to join a highly skilled occupation, becoming a manager (ISCO 1), professional (ISCO 2) or technician or associated professional (ISCO 3). Figure 1.2 shows that, on average across the 32 countries, more than 80% of students aspire to work in a high-skilled profession, of whom 62% as a professional, 6% as a senior official or manager, and 12% as a technician or associated professional. All these professions require at least some level of tertiary education as per the ILO classification (ILO, 2012). What is remarkable is that students' preferred occupations are stable across regions and countries. Brazil and Liberia are the only two countries where fewer than half of students wish to work in top-skilled occupations (managers and professionals), and the share is just below 50%.

Figure 1.1. **A large share of students would like to work in the public sector (%)**

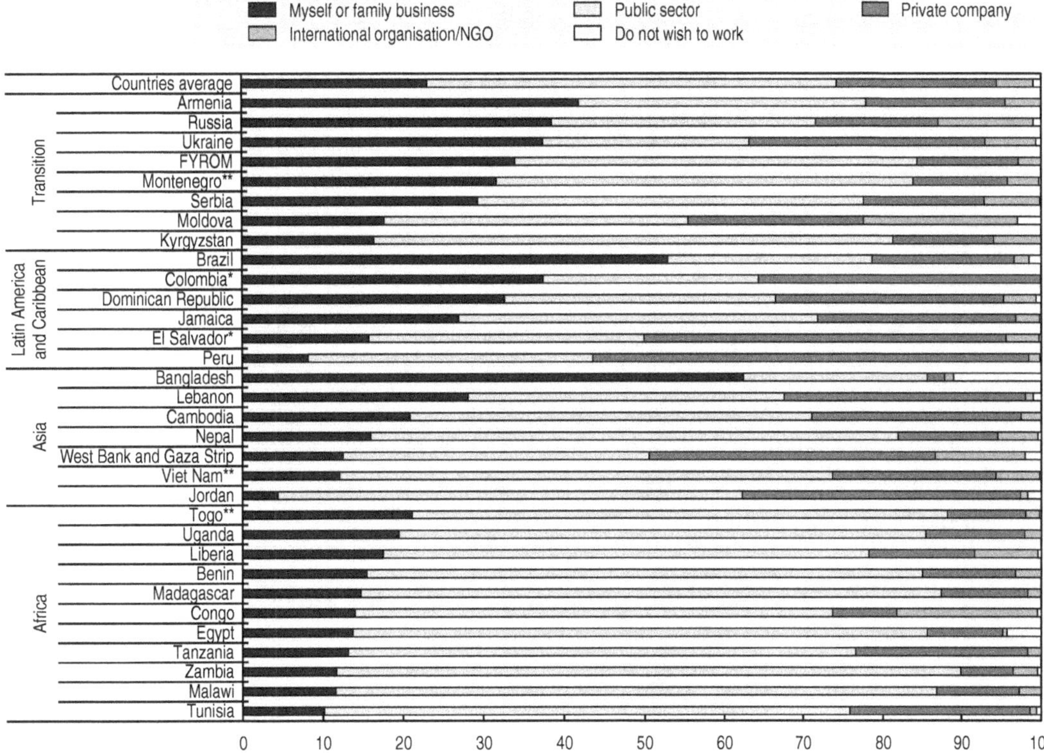

Note: The figure represents the distribution of answer from students who were asked: "Ideally, who would you like to work for?" Within each region, countries are sorted by the share of students wishing to work for themselves or a family business. FYROM corresponds to Former Yugoslav Republic of Macedonia.

* Data for Colombia and El Salvador refer to the urban population only.

** Estimations for Montenegro, Togo and Viet Nam do not account for sampling weights as they are missing in the data.

Source: Own calculations based on School-to-Work Transition Surveys 2012-2015, ILO.

Few students express the wish to work in intermediate-skilled occupations such as clerical support, services, sales or crafts. An average of just 14% of the students surveyed chose services, trade or craft as their preferred future occupation. Service jobs hold greatest appeal for Colombian and Jamaican students (15%), while crafts and related occupations are most attractive to students in Moldova (15%) and the Former Yugoslav Republic of Macedonia (FYROM, 19%). The data further reveal that fewer than 1% of students aspire to become skilled agricultural workers, while only 1.4% aspire to become plant operators or assembly lines workers in the industrial sector, even though such activities are often considered to be an important engine for growth in developing countries (Figure 1.2).

Box 1.1. **The ILO's School-to-Work Transition Surveys**

In an effort to fill the information gap on relevant labour market insights on young people, notably in terms of transition from school to stable employment, the ILO – with financial support of the Master Card Foundation – implemented the Work4Youth project to collect comparable and exhaustive labour market surveys in more than 30 developing and emerging countries.

This study relies on an analysis of School-to-Work Transition Surveys (SWTS) collected between 2012 and 2015 in 32 developing countries. The data are nationally representative of young people aged 15 to 29, except in Colombia and El Salvador, where only urban areas are covered, and Brazil, where the data cover only 10 regions. The data document the transition of the youth to the labour market. As such, SWTS are youth-specific labour market surveys with modules asking questions on the educational background of each participant, the current labour market situation and retrospective data on past career choices. The countries and years of survey used in the report are as follows:

Year of survey	Countries
2012	Peru and the Russian Federation
2013	Bangladesh, Brazil, Colombia, Dominican Republic, Kyrgyzstan, Montenegro, Nepal, Tanzania and Tunisia
2014	Armenia, Cambodia, Egypt, El Salvador, Liberia, Former Yugoslav Republic of Macedonia, Malawi, Togo and Zambia
2015	Republic of the Congo, Jamaica, Jordan, Lebanon, Madagascar, Moldova, West Bank and Gaza Strip, Serbia, Uganda and Ukraine

Throughout the analysis, the results at the country level are displayed according to United Nations classification as follows:

Region	Countries
Africa	Benin, Republic of the Congo, Egypt, Liberia, Madagascar, Malawi, Tanzania, Togo, Uganda and Zambia
Asia	Bangladesh, Cambodia, Nepal, Viet Nam, Jordan, Lebanon, West Bank and Gaza Strip
Latin America and Caribbean	Brazil, Colombia, Dominican Republic, El Salvador, Jamaica, Peru
Transition countries	Armenia, Kyrgyzstan, Former Yugoslav Republic of Macedonia, Moldova, Montenegro, Russian Federation, Serbia, Ukraine

Use of the data for descriptive statistics

The descriptive statistics are calculated based only on the data from the latest available round of the SWTS in order to provide up-to-date results. When possible, the statistical analysis used analytical weights for the calculations. Yet, weights were not available for Montenegro, Togo and Viet Nam, and consequently the estimations presented for these countries do not take into account any weights (these countries are highlighted by a * in the figures).

In the report, "Countries average" refers to the simple mean of all countries' statistics displayed, regardless of weight availability and national representativeness. Colombia and El Salvador are marked with "**" to indicate that the statistics computed are only representative of the urban population.

All statistics related to career aspirations are computed on the 15-29-year-old population currently enrolled at any level of education (as only this population was asked about their ideal sector and occupation). The rest of the analysis relies on the 15-29-year-old working population.

Use of the data for the regression analysis

For the purpose of the regression analysis, and to increase statistical power, all available SWTS rounds are used. The use of weights is similar to the method used in the descriptive statistics. Country-level regressions use analytical weights in general and no weights for Montenegro, Viet Nam and Togo.

Box 1.1. The ILO's School-to-Work Transition Surveys (cont.)

Additionally, for the regression pooling, weights of all countries combined (labelled as "Overall" in the figures and tables) are not used, as this would imply dropping Viet Nam, Montenegro and Togo from the analysis. Please note that the conclusions hold when weights are included and Viet Nam, Montenegro and Togo are excluded from the analysis.

Sources:
ILO (2009a), "*Module 1: Basic concepts, role and implementation process*", in ILO School-to-Work Transition Survey: A Methodological Guide, International Labour Office, Geneva.
ILO (2009b), "*Module 3: Sampling methodology*", in ILO School-to-Work Transition Survey: A Methodological Guide, International Labour Office, Geneva.
More detailed information is available here: www.ilo.org/employment/areas/youth-employment/work-for-youth/WCMS_191853/lang--en/index.html.

Figure 1.2. A large share of 15-29-year-old students would like to work in a high-skilled occupation (%)

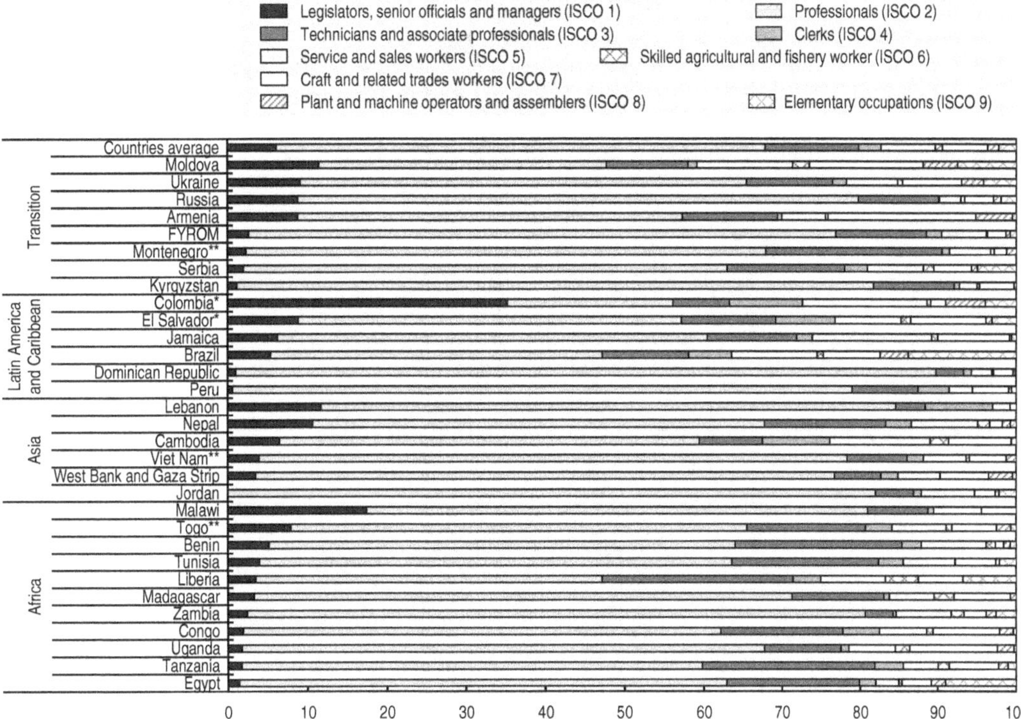

Note: The figure represents the distribution of answer from students who were asked: "Ideally, what type of work would you like to do?" Occupation categories correspond to the nine major groups under the International Statistical Classification of Occupation (ISCO-08). Within each region, countries are sorted by the proportion of 15-29-year-old students wishing to work as legislators, senior officials or managers. Data are not available for Bangladesh. FYROM corresponds to Former Yugoslav Republic of Macedonia.

* Data for Colombia and El Salvador refer to the urban population only.

** Estimations for Montenegro, Togo and Viet Nam do not account for sampling weights as they are missing in the data.

Source: Own calculations based on School-to-Work Transition Surveys 2012-2015, ILO.

Box 1.2. **Key definitions**

Adjusted measure of satisfaction

The subjective measure of job satisfaction in SWTS data is measured by asking young workers to what extent they are satisfied with their main job. They can select the following options: very satisfied, somewhat satisfied, somewhat unsatisfied, and very unsatisfied. Additionally, the questionnaire includes a yes/no question about the attitude of young workers regarding their job, asking them whether they would like to change their current employment situation. The adjusted measure of satisfaction used in this report combined both variables to construct a dummy variable equal to 1 if a young worker is very or somewhat satisfied and not wanting to change jobs, and 0 when this is not case.

Employment status

The SWTS generic questionnaire provides information about the employment status of young workers by asking them to describe their job/activity among the following categories: employee (working for someone else for pay in cash or in kind), employer (employing one or more employees), own-account worker (not employing any employee), member of a producers' co-operative, helping without pay in the business or farm of another household/family member. Due to the relatively low sample size for some of these options (employer, co-operative member) and to differences across countries, we aggregated these categories into three groups: wage employees, self-employed (including employers, own-account workers and co-operative members) and unpaid family workers (corresponding to helping without pay).

Career aspirations

In the report, career aspirations are documented via two questions asked to 15-29-year-old students enrolled at any level of education. The first – "Ideally, what type of work would you like to do?" – concerns occupations and uses the ISCO as a reference. The second – "Ideally, who would you like to work for?" – concerns sectors of activity. In response to the second question, the students had to choose one of the following options: myself (own business/farm), work for the government/public sector, work for a private company, work for an international or non-profit organisation, work for family business/farm, do not wish to work. The options were aggregated into self-employment (myself, work for family business/farm), public sector (including international and non-profit organisations) and private sector. Students unwilling to work were discarded from the sample as they represented a negligible proportion of individuals.

Self-concept factors exert a strong influence on youth career aspirations

Self-concept factors are factors that influence the way one sees oneself and often relate to demographic or family characteristics, socio-economic status and academic performance. There are many channels through which self-concept factors can influence career aspirations. Gender stereotypes, culture, community and family shape aspirations through the transmission of values, the provision of role models or the imposition of rewards and punishments for following or not following specific paths. Another potential channel is information. Youth from different groups (in terms instance of location, income status and parents' education, for instance) might have access to a different set of information about what is possible, or not, for them to achieve through life. Aspirations could also simply result from groups' preferences and reflect their optimal professional and societal outcome. These channels are not mutually exclusive and there are many other ways in which these characteristics could be linked to aspirations. Based on descriptive statistics and multivariate analysis for 32 countries, this section identifies which factors have the greatest influence on youth career aspirations and which have the least influence.

High student career expectations in developing countries must be seen in the light of the fact that many young people today are more educated than their fathers. The SWTS data show that, on average across the 32 countries, around 37% of young workers have completed a higher level of education than their fathers, while 45% have reached the same level and 18% experienced a downward evolution (Figure 1.3). The upward education mobility is striking in LAC and Asian countries, where respectively 50% and 44% of young people have a higher level of education than their fathers. In these regions, upward mobility is also significantly more frequent than downward mobility in most cases. Jordan, West Bank and Gaza Strip, and the Russian Federation are remarkable exceptions, as they constitute the few countries where downward education mobility is much more frequent than upward mobility. In Zambia, Liberia and the Republic of the Congo (Congo), downward mobility is also more common than upward mobility, but the differences are small.

Figure 1.3. **Many young workers in developing countries have experienced upward education mobility (%)**

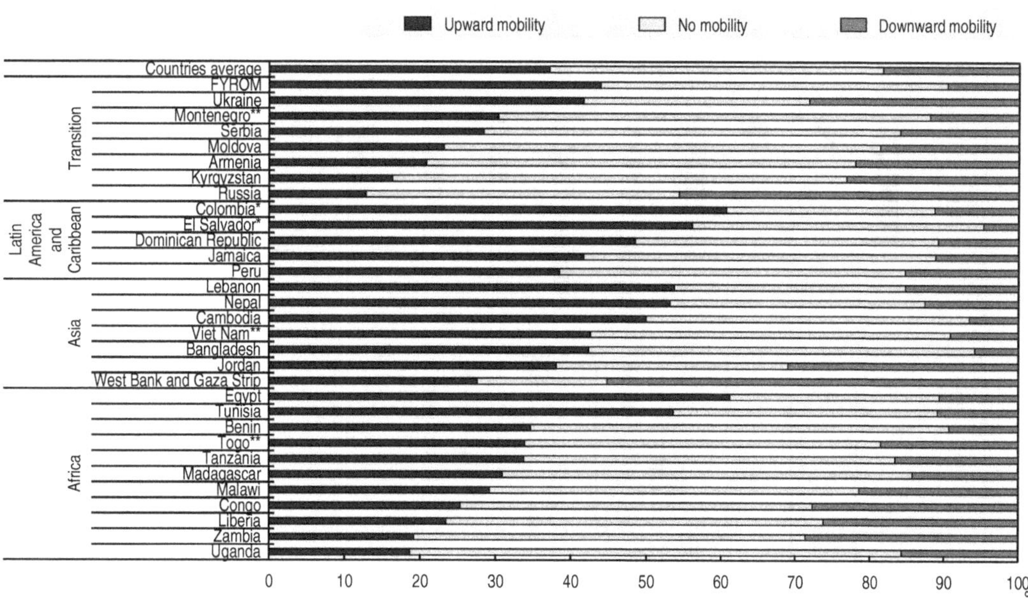

Notes: Upward mobility in terms of education refers to any case in which an individual has completed a higher education level than her/his father and downward mobility refers to a situation in which an individual's father completed a higher education level. Within each region, countries are sorted by the proportion of young workers having experienced upward mobility. Data are not available for Brazil. FYROM corresponds to Former Yugoslav Republic of Macedonia.

* Data for Colombia and El Salvador refer to the urban population only.

** Estimations for Montenegro, Togo and Viet Nam do not account for sampling weights as they are missing in the data.

Source: Own calculations based on School-to-Work Transition Surveys 2012-2015, ILO.

Women and disadvantaged students are more likely to be attracted by the public sector and less by self-employment. Women and students from rural areas, from a poorer background and with less educated fathers are more likely to want to work in the public sector and less likely to favour self-employment (Figure 1.4). The probability of wanting to work in the private sector is also significantly lower for students in rural areas, but not for women or students from poor backgrounds. Noticeably, the link between education and a desire to work in the public sector vanishes as the father's education level becomes higher. Students whose fathers have completed a tertiary degree are more likely to want to work in the private sector and not in the public sector. This might reflect greater confidence among a certain elite about the possibility of thriving in private companies. What is also worth noting is that the father's occupation has no clear influence on students' desire to work in one or another sector (Figure 1.4).[1]

Figure 1.4. The public sector appeals more than the private sector to students from a lower socio-economic background

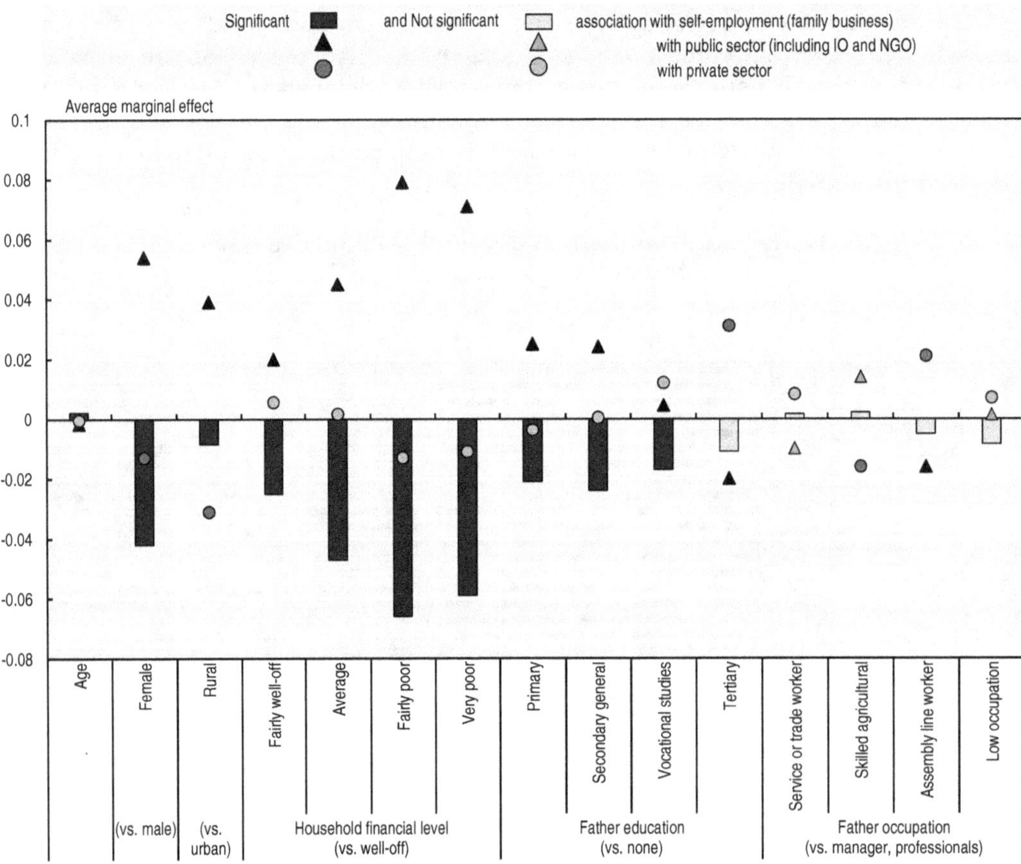

Notes: The figure displays the average marginal effect of each of the characteristics on the probability that a young person wants to work in a given sector of activity, estimated from a multinomial logit model including all countries, country and year fixed effects, whether the respondent suffers from at least one health issue and the level of study he/she is currently attending as additional explanatory variables not reported here. The figure reads as follows: living in a rural area is associated with an increase of 0.046 of the probability of wishing to work in the public sector compared to living in an urban setting. Estimated associations that are significantly different from 0 (at the 95% confidence level) are represented in a darker tone.

Source: Own calculations based on School-to-Work Transition Surveys 2012-2015, ILO.

Students from rural areas and from low-income households are more often attracted by less skilled occupations. These students, with a less-educated background, are less likely to aspire to work in a highly skilled occupation (Figure 1.5). The link between the self-declared poverty level and the desire to work in a medium- or low-skilled occupation is particularly striking. In comparison to students who consider themselves to be well-off, the probability of aiming at a high-skilled occupation decreases continuously with the household poverty level.

Women with a highly educated father show a strong preference for highly skilled occupations. The results show a clear distaste among women for low-skilled occupations. Moreover, the more educated the father, the more likely the student is to wish for a job in a high-skilled occupation.

Students' occupational preferences and fathers' occupations are closely correlated. Students seem to be attracted by the occupation of their fathers. Children of fathers working in a medium- or low-skilled occupation are more likely to say they want to work in, respectively, a medium- or low-skilled occupation than students whose fathers work in a high-skilled occupation.

Figure 1.5. **Students from a lower socio-economic background have lower professional aspirations**

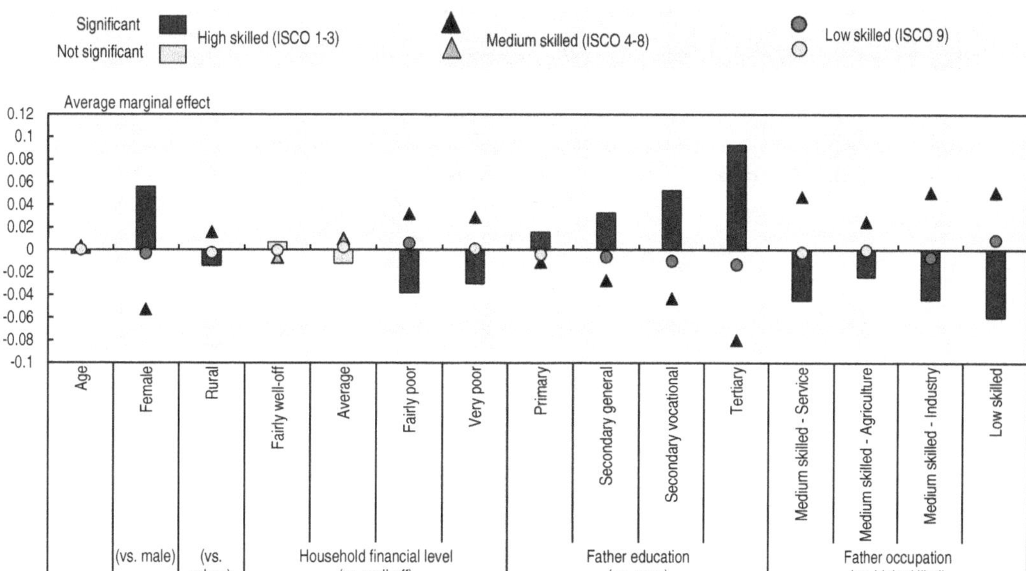

Note: The figure displays the average marginal effect of each of the characteristics on the probability that a young person wants to work at a given occupation classified by skill levels, estimated from a multinomial logit model including all countries, country and year fixed effects, whether the respondent suffers from at least one health issue and the level of study he/she is currently attending as additional explanatory variables not reported here. The figure reads as follows: having a father working in a low-skilled occupation is associated with an increase of 0.13 of the probability of wanting to work in a low-skilled activity compared to having a father working in a high-skilled occupation. Estimated associations that are significantly different from 0 (at the 95% confidence level) are represented in a darker tone.

Source: Own calculations based on School-to-Work Transition Surveys 2012-2015, ILO.

By and large, young people seem to adapt their career aspirations to their social position, with the noticeable exception of female students, who have high career aspirations. Students are indeed more likely to wish to work at the same level of occupation as their fathers, and students from poorer or less-educated backgrounds are less likely to aspire to high-skilled occupations.[2] However, female students are more likely than young men to be attracted by high-skilled occupations. All in all, these findings indicate that young men from different categories tend to adapt their career aspirations to their social position. The extent to which youth aspirations are aligned with the reality of labour markets in developing countries remains to be investigated, however.

Notes

1. Using the mother's education level instead of the father's does not modify the conclusion, but young people whose mothers are not working in agriculture are clearly less likely to want to work in the public sector than those with a mother working in agriculture.
2. The conclusion also holds when the mother's education level and occupation are taken into account.

References

AfDB/OECD/UNDP/UNECA (2012), *African Economic Outlook 2012: Promoting Youth Employment*, OECD Publishing, Paris, http://dx.doi.org/10.1787/aeo-2012-en.

ILO (2015), *School-to-Work Transition Surveys*, International Labour Organization, Geneva, www.ilo.org/employment/areas/youth-employment/work-for-youth/WCMS_191853/lang--en/index.htm.

ILO (2012), International Standard Classification of Occupations, Classification Structure (Part 2) and Group definitions (Part 3). ISCO-08, Vol. 1, International Labour Organization, Geneva, www.ilo.org/public/english/bureau/stat/isco/isco08/.

ILO (2009a), "Module 1: Basic concepts, role and implementation process", *School-To-Work Transition Survey: A Methodological Guide*, International Labour Organization, Geneva, www.ilo.org/employment/Whatwedo/Instructionmaterials/WCMS_140857/lang--en/index.htm.

ILO (2009b), "Module 3: Sampling methodology", *ILO School-To-Work Transition Survey: A Methodological Guide*, International Labour Organization, Geneva, www.ilo.org/employment/areas/youth-employment/work-for-youth/WCMS_191853/lang--en/index.htm.

Chapter 2

Facets of job satisfaction in developing countries

Job satisfaction is a common measurement of subjective well-being in the world of work, one that can be assessed both at the overall level and at the facet level. Job facet satisfaction concerns the extent to which an individual is satisfied with different aspects of the job. Measurement of job facet satisfaction helps identify what actually matters for people in terms of job characteristics and employment conditions. This chapter provides an assessment of the different aspects of the job that young people value and that bring greater job satisfaction. It shows that facets of job satisfaction can add to our understanding of job quality. It further discusses the reasons for using an adjusted measure of job satisfaction.

Traditional approaches to the measurement of job quality rely on objective indicators that influence well-being. Job quality covers multiple dimensions of employment, ranging from traditional factors such as earnings, working time, benefits and job security to less tangible characteristics including the quality of the relationship with colleagues and hierarchy, the variety of tasks and responsibilities, or the autonomy of decision making (Stiglitz Sen and Fitoussi, 2009). While researchers and practitioners agree on the multi-dimensional nature of employment quality, various measurement frameworks coexist, highlighting different aspects of employment quality and relying on different types of indicators. Existing frameworks share a common feature: they rely on objective indicators of the labour market that have been shown to influence people's well-being. Some frameworks, such as the ILO framework on measuring decent work (ILO, 2008) and the OECD's Job Quality Framework, include several indicators that are meant to capture different dimensions of job quality (OECD, 2014, 2015, 2017b). In contrast, the framework of the European Foundation for the Improvement of Living and Working Conditions (Eurofound) focuses on a limited set of individual level indicators in order to cover specifically workers' well-being (Eurofound, 2012).

Evidence, mostly from OECD countries, highlights the importance of several job characteristics for people's well-being. A large body of literature documents the link between the set of indicators usually selected in labour-market quality measurement frameworks and people's well-being. Not having a job appears to be the main source of low well-being for individuals (Clark, 2010; Latif, 2010; Dolan Peasgood and White, 2008; McKee-Ryan et al., 2005; Blanchflower and Oswald, 2002; Theodossiou, 1998). People's subjective well-being is also very much related to the quality and attributes of their jobs. For example, workers with higher earnings are generally more satisfied with their lives (Deaton and Kahneman, 2010; Sacks Stevenson and Wolfers, 2012; Stevenson and Wolfers, 2008 and 2013). Yet, individuals' well-being is also sensitive to the distribution of earnings in the society (Senik, 2009; Ferrer-i-Carbonell and Ramos, 2010; Clark and D'Ambrosio, 2014), and particularly to the relative position of their earnings to those of others (Card et al, 2012, Clark et al., 2008). Improved labour-market security also contributes to workers' well-being. A higher risk of unemployment is negatively correlated with well-being (Green, 2011), as is the length of unemployment spells (Hijzen and Menyhert, 2016). Finally, work environment factors – such as the degree of autonomy and control, work load, workplace organisation or personal relationship with colleagues and management – have been shown to affect health and well-being (OECD, 2012 and 2013).

The link between employment characteristics and youth well-being in low- and middle-income countries must be uncovered to support a well-informed policy dialogue on job quality that can be relevant to countries at different stages of development. Most of the evidence on the link between employment characteristics and well-being covers OECD countries. Research covering low-income countries mainly investigates the link between income and well-being (Clark and Senik, 2010). Some studies document the impact of the level and relative distribution of earnings on job satisfaction in China (Gao and Smyth, 2010; Knight and Gunatilaka, 2010a and 2010b) or the role of subjective poverty in Malawi (Ravallion and Lokshin, 2010), but few studies look at job quality. One notable exception is Falco and Haywood (2013), which shows considerable heterogeneity in the subjective well-being of Ghanaian workers depending on their sectors and status of employment, using panel data. While it is likely that a number of job characteristics affect workers in a similar way across the world, there is no reason to consider that the relative importance of job-related determinants of job satisfaction are similar across countries at different stages of development.

Facets of job satisfaction add to the understanding of job quality

This chapter explores which job characteristic in low- and middle-income countries is valued by young people and results in greater job satisfaction. Facets of job refer to feelings about specific job aspects, such as salary, benefits, work hierarchy (reporting structure), growth opportunities, work environment and the quality of relationships with co-workers (Mueller and Kim, 2008). Measurements of job facet satisfaction allow identification of what really matters to workers in terms of job characteristics and employment conditions; they also make it possible to isolate specific aspects of a job that correlate with job satisfaction. The findings may help firms improve overall job satisfaction or understand organisational challenges such as high turnover (Kerber and Campbell, 1987). They are equally important for policy makers, who may, for instance, use job facet satisfaction results to engage in labour-market and labour-code reforms, or to adapt international job quality frameworks to their specific countries. The analysis performed in this chapter takes into account developing countries' labour-market characteristics, such as the existence of unpaid family workers, the prevalence of self-employment, a large and persistent informal sector, or the lack of unemployment and health benefits, among other factors.

Despite the inherent advantages of using job satisfaction measures to document job quality and employment preferences, limitations exist, and this demands careful interpretation of the findings. Self-reported satisfaction measures have been widely used in the literature and their properties widely discussed (Kahneman and Krueger, 2006). The main advantage of subjective well-being measures is their simplicity, and their main virtue is to allow synthesising multi-faceted aspects of situations in a coherent way regarding the respondent. As such, they provide a broader perspective. There is a consensus that such measures are not simply noise but reflect meaningful information, which provides valid and reliable comparisons across people, countries and over time (Nikolova, 2016; OECD, 2011). An additional valuable property of self-reported satisfaction measures, which has often been highlighted, is their democratic and non-paternalistic nature, as they allow respondents to express their own judgement (Binder, 2014). Yet there is a down side to the use of job satisfaction as measure of well-being. For example, individuals' assessments of their satisfaction in life can vary according to the time of the day when they were asked the question or due to micro-events (Kahneman and Krueger, 2006). The limited scale (from 1 to 4) on which job satisfaction is recorded in the analysis, even if commonly used, also reduces the possibility to capture variations in people's satisfaction. Other challenges are presented by hedonic adaptation, or the fact that people's judgement about their satisfaction level adjusts to circumstances over time and according to what appears possible, and social comparison, or the fact that people tend to formulate a judgement on their level of satisfaction based on their relative position in comparison to a reference group. However, assuming that well-being is sufficiently correlated with preference satisfaction, it is reasonable to believe that young people who are satisfied with their job will experience greater well-being (Angner, 2012).

Facets of job satisfaction are derived from an adjusted measure of job satisfaction

Facets of job satisfaction are derived from the statistical correlation between an adjusted measure of job satisfaction and a set of employment characteristics, controlling for other socio-demographic factors. The analysis of job facet satisfaction is based on two self-declared measures related to the respondents' employment situation: i) a categorical variable recording the degree of satisfaction of young workers over four categories (very satisfied, somewhat satisfied, somewhat dissatisfied and very dissatisfied); and ii) a dummy variable that provides information on whether the worker wants to change his/her employment situation or not. A more restrictive measure of job satisfaction is then computed based on the assumption that satisfied individuals are those who are satisfied or very satisfied with their job and do not wish to change their current employment situation. Correlations between this adjusted measure of satisfaction and a set of job related characteristics measuring the employment situation (types of employment, employment status, industry and occupations) and more qualitative aspects of the jobs (type of contract, earnings, job security, informality, etc.) are then derived from multivariate country-level analysis, controlling for individual and household characteristics. In order to increase the statistical power, the analysis is complemented with a pooled regression with all countries, controlling for country and year fixed effects.[1]

Control variables such as wealth and education affect job satisfaction. The statistical analysis is conducted for all young workers, and then separately for male, female, urban and rural youth workers to account for possible heterogeneity in the way the individual characteristics may influence job satisfaction. The results on the control variables show that levels of job satisfaction are similar among men and women and among rural and urban youth workers in most countries. At the same time, young workers who belong to poorer households and those who are most highly educated report lower levels of job satisfaction on average.

Measurement consistency is improved by using a more restrictive measure of job satisfaction that exploits information about people's desire to change jobs. Adjusting raw measures of job satisfaction in the School-to-Work Transition Surveys (SWTS) is desirable, since some workers (28%) who say they are satisfied or very satisfied with their jobs would also like to change their employment situation (Annex 2.A1, Figure 2.A1.1). Of these, 75% wish to change jobs to improve their employment situation, while 25% would like a change because their job is temporary or they fear losing it, suggesting that these workers may not be "truly" satisfied with their employment situation (Annex 2.A1, Figure 2.A1.2). Further investigation does indeed indicate that there is a strong negative correlation between the desire to change jobs and the degree of satisfaction of young workers. The average marginal effects from a Probit regression of a dummy equal to one if the worker wishes to change jobs at the different levels of satisfaction are reported in Annex 2.A1, Figure 2.A1.3, Panel A. Additional controls include age, gender and whether the young worker lives in an urban or rural setting. The results are very consistent across countries and indicate that the higher the satisfaction level, the lower the probability that an individual would want to change jobs. Higher job satisfaction is also associated with a lower probability of actively looking for an alternative job (Annex 2.A1, Figure 2.A1.3, Panel B). The more satisfied the young workers, the less likely they are to undertake the steps needed to find a new job. Overall, these findings indicate that using a more restrictive measure of job satisfaction – one that defines job satisfaction as those individuals who are somewhat satisfied or very satisfied with their job and who do not wish to change their current employment situation – is more satisfactory.

When a more restrictive definition of satisfaction is used, far fewer young workers appear to be truly satisfied. On average across the 32 countries, 80% of young workers say they are satisfied with their jobs, but only half say they are not only satisfied but also do not wish to change their current employment situation (Figure 2.1). In other words, there is a considerable margin of young people who do not appear to be truly satisfied, since despite expressing job satisfaction, they also say they would like to change jobs. Moreover, there is widespread heterogeneity across countries as to the effect of using an adjusted measure of job satisfaction instead of the crude measure. Latin American and the Caribbean (LAC) and African countries are more affected by the use of different definitions. In countries such as Peru, Salvador, Zambia or the Republic of the Congo

(Congo), using a more restrictive measure decreases the share of satisfied individuals by more than half. The difference is relatively small in Asia (except for Cambodia) and transition economies.

Figure 2.1. **Share of satisfied young workers, using a raw and adjusted measure, %**

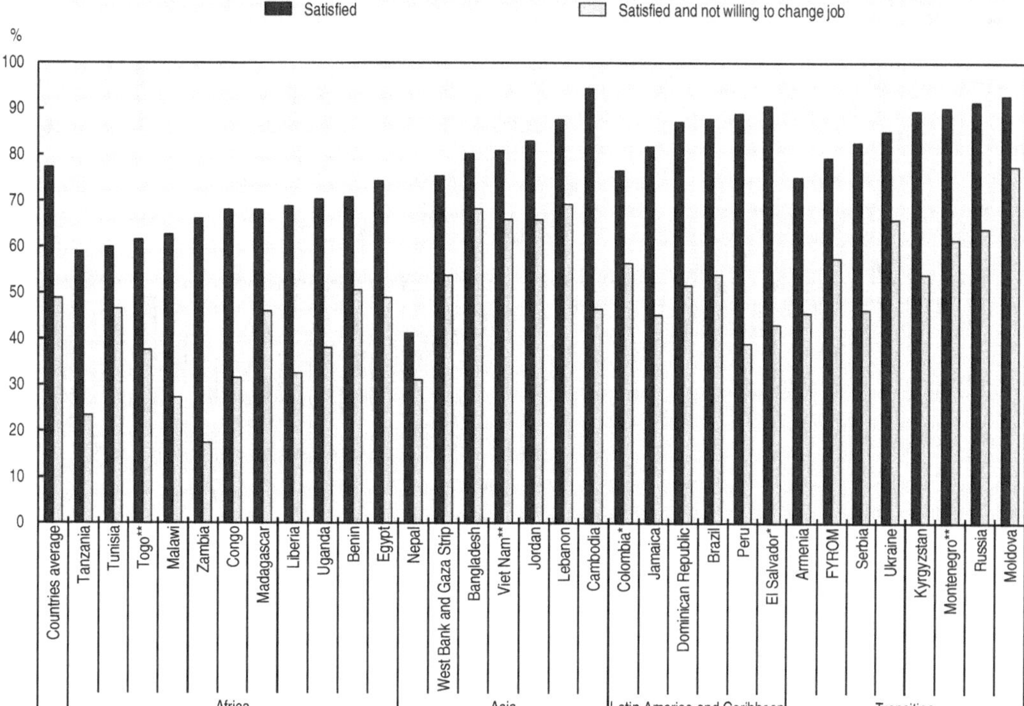

Note: Within each region, countries are sorted by the proportion of young workers satisfied with their job.
* Data for Colombia and El Salvador refer to the urban population only. FYROM corresponds to Former Yugoslav Republic of Macedonia.
** Estimations for Montenegro, Togo and Viet Nam do not account for sampling weights as they are missing in the data.
Source: Own calculations based on School-to-Work Transition Surveys 2012-2015, ILO.

Many key job characteristics are associated with greater job satisfaction[2]

Compared to wage employment, self-employment is a strong driver of job satisfaction among young workers across nearly all countries, but only when it is by choice or required by the family and not for lack of other employment possibilities. This indicates that employment status matters for young people's well-being. Overall, compared to wage employment, being self-employed by choice (workers who choose this status for greater independence, higher income or flexibility in working time) or because it is required by the family significantly increases the probability being satisfied, while being self-employed due to the lack of wage employment decreases the probability of being satisfied (Figure 2.2, Panel A). Recent evidence from developing countries shows that only a tiny portion of youth entrepreneurs prove to be successful and that a large number are confined to subsistence activities (OECD, 2017a). Similarly, engaging in unpaid family work to learn the family business or because it is required by the family is in general associated with a higher probability of satisfaction compared to wage employment, even though the difference is not statistically significant overall (Figure 2.2, Panel B). However, being an unpaid family worker due to lack of wage employment opportunities significantly reduces the probability of being satisfied.

Figure 2.2. **Self-employment raises job satisfaction relative to wage employment, but not when it is by default**

Panel A. Drivers of self-employment

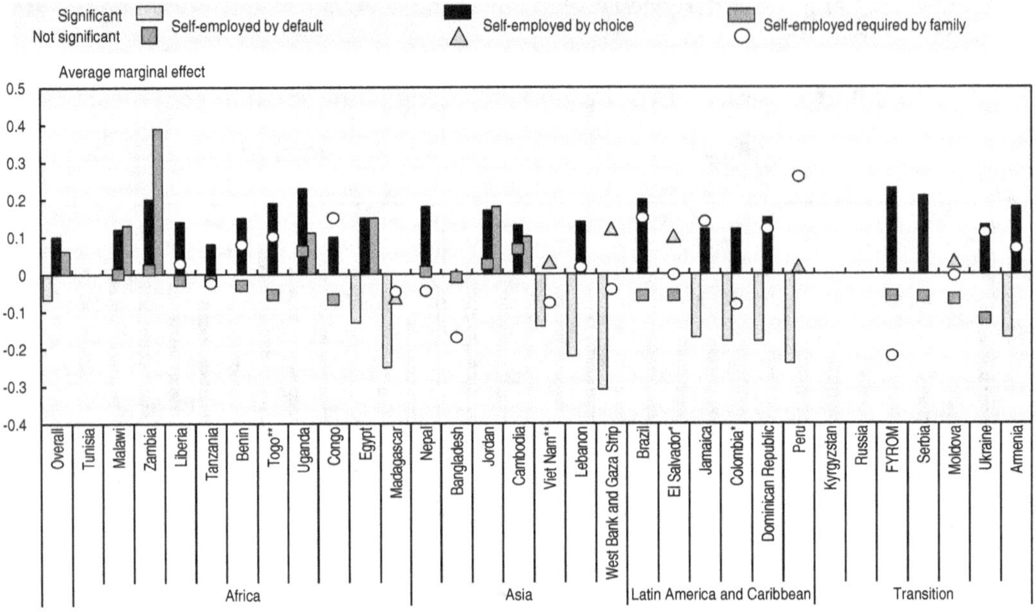

Panel B. Drivers of unpaid family work

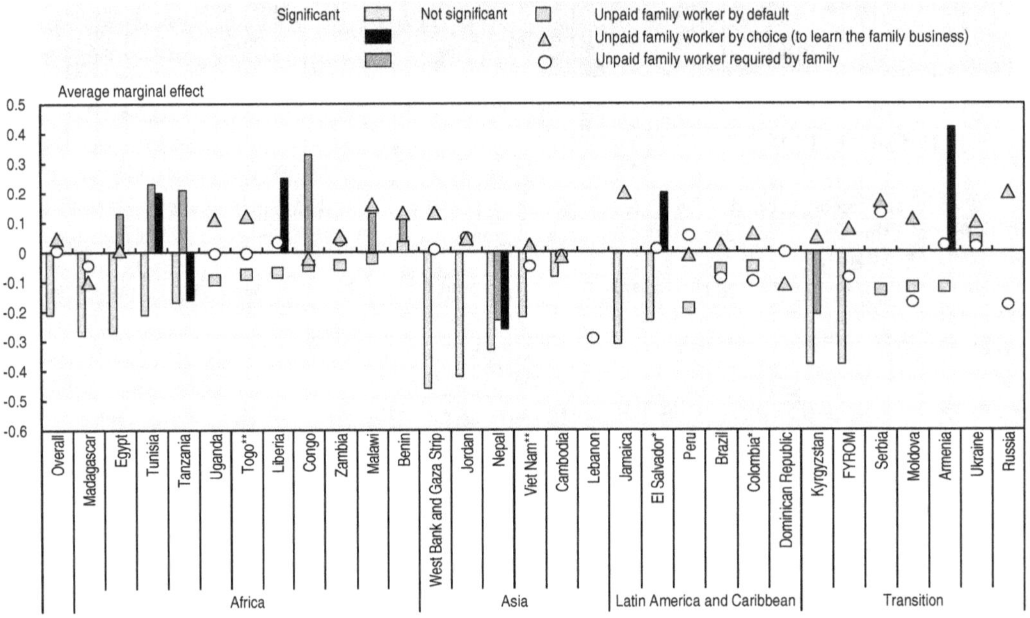

Note: The figure displays the average marginal effect of each employment status on the probability of being satisfied and not wishing to change jobs (i.e. the adjusted measure of satisfaction), compared to being wage employed. The average marginal effects are estimated from a Probit model similar to the one described in Annex 2.A2 (and displayed in Tables 2.A2.1, 2.A2.2 and 2.A2.3) with the only difference being that standardised monthly income is not included here in order to examine the association between being an unpaid family worker and job satisfaction, while the model in Annex 2.A2 only focuses on wage employees and self-employed. The figure reads as follows: being an unpaid family worker by choice in Liberia is associated with an increase of 0.25 of the probability of being satisfied with the current job (adjusted measure) compared to being wage employed, everything else being equal. Estimated associations that are significantly different from 0 (at the 95% confidence level) are represented in a darker tone. Estimations from Montenegro (Panels A and B) and Bangladesh (Panel B) are missing due to the lack of data. FYROM corresponds to Former Yugoslav Republic of Macedonia.

* Data for Colombia and El Salvador refer to the urban population only.

** Estimations for Montenegro, Togo and Viet Nam do not account for sampling weights as they are missing in the data.

Source: Own calculations based on School-to-Work Transition Surveys 2012-2015, ILO.

Low-skilled occupations are associated with a lower level of job satisfaction in all countries, and the same is true of medium-skilled occupations in transition countries and Latin America. Overall, young workers, especially male workers, who are engaged in low-skilled occupations are much less likely to be satisfied with their jobs than workers engaged in high-skilled activities, everything else being equal (Figure 2.3, Panel A). This is also true at the country level in all regions, and is most pronounced in African and transition economies. Working in a low-skilled occupation is particularly detrimental to satisfaction in countries like Congo and Egypt, Bangladesh and Viet Nam, and in transition economies such as Ukraine, Kyrgyzstan and Russian Federation. Medium-skilled occupations are associated with less satisfaction in general, and particularly transition countries.

In comparison to other industries, working in agriculture reduces job satisfaction. Young workers in sectors other than agriculture are more often satisfied with their work than those engaged in agricultural activities (Figure 2.3, Panel B). This is particularly the case for workers engaged in manufacturing activities and in information, communication and financial and other services. The correlation between working in manufacturing and industrial activities and job satisfaction is particularly strong in Africa and transition economies. While working in wholesale and retail trade or transportation is also positively associated with job satisfaction in comparison to agricultural work, the link is weaker and actually not significant when disaggregated occupations are included in the regression. Yet it remains significantly associated with higher satisfaction in many African and transition countries. For female young workers, moreover, working in manufacturing does not increase job satisfaction compared to working in agriculture (Annex 2.A2, Table 2.A2.4).

Figure 2.3. **The skills level of occupations and sector of activity affect workers' job satisfaction**

Panel A. Occupation by level of qualification

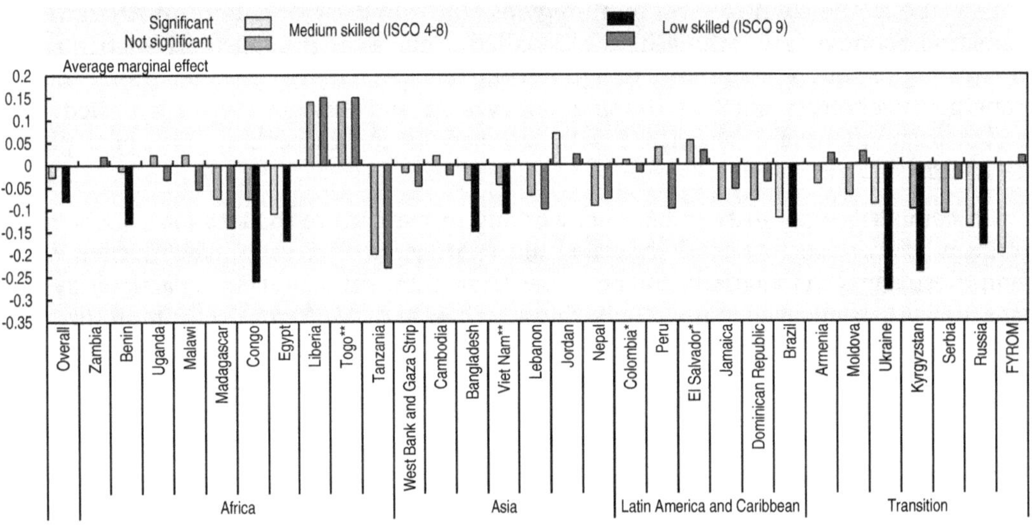

Panel B. Sectors of activity

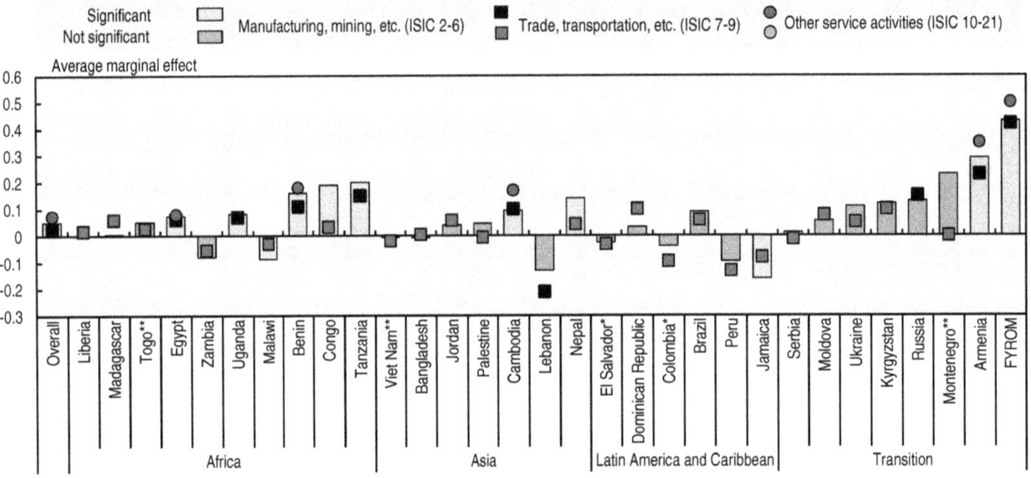

Note: The figure displays the average marginal effect of being engaged in a low- or medium-skilled occupation compared to a high-skilled occupation (Panel A), and the average marginal effect of working in various sectors of activity (or industries) compared to agriculture (Panel B), on the probability of being satisfied and not wishing to change jobs (i.e. the adjusted measure of satisfaction). The skill level of occupations is based on the ISCO. Sectors are aggregated in four categories based on the International Standard Industry Classification (ISIC): agriculture, etc. (ISIC 1), the reference category; manufacturing, mining, etc. (ISIC 2-6); trade, transportation etc. (ISCI 7-9); and other services (ISIC 10 to 21). The average marginal effects are estimated from the Probit model described in Annex 2.A2 and displayed in Tables 2.A2.1, 2.A2.2 and 2.A2.3. The figure reads as follows: Working in a low-skilled occupation in Benin is associated with a decrease of 0.13 of the probability of being satisfied with the current job (adjusted measure) in comparison to working in a high-skilled occupation, everything else being equal. Estimated associations that are significantly different from 0 (at the 95% confidence level) are represented in a darker tone. Estimations from Tunisia (Panels A and B) and Montenegro (Panel A) are missing due to the lack of data. FYROM corresponds to Former Yugoslav Republic of Macedonia.

* Data for Colombia and El Salvador refer to the urban population only.

** Estimations for Montenegro, Togo and Viet Nam do not account for sampling weights as they are missing in the data.

Source: Own calculations based on School-to-Work Transition Surveys 2012-2015, ILO.

Informality matters in all countries, with young people who work in an unregistered activity tending to be less satisfied with their jobs. This correlation probably captures the fact that workers in the informal economy experience worse working conditions. The results are consistent across countries (Figure 2.4), and the conclusion holds true for rural and urban youth, and for female and male workers. Interestingly, both wage employees and self-employed workers display lower job satisfaction when they work in an unregistered business.

Figure 2.4. **Working in an unregistered activity decreases job satisfaction**

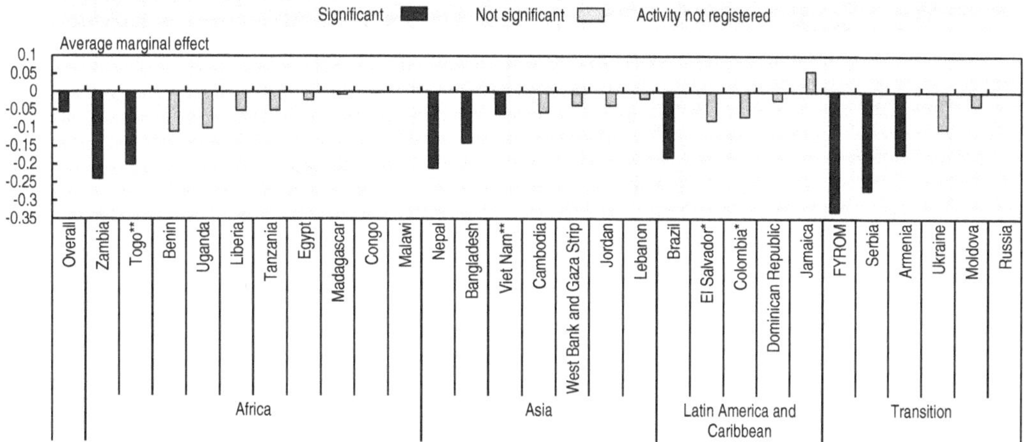

Note: The figure displays the average marginal effect of working in an unregistered activity in comparison to a registered one on the probability of being satisfied and not wishing to change jobs (i.e. the adjusted measure of satisfaction). The average marginal effects are estimated the Probit model described in Annex 2.A2 and displayed in Tables 2.A2.1, 2.A2.2 and 2.A2.3. The figure reads as follows: Working in an unregistered activity in Nepal is associated with a decrease of 0.21 of the probability of being satisfied with the current job (adjusted measure) in comparison to working in a registered activity, everything else being equal. Estimated associations that are significantly different from 0 (at the 95% confidence level) are represented in a darker tone. Estimations from Kyrgyzstan, Peru and Tunisia are missing due to the lack of data, and the estimate for Montenegro reaches -2.4 (and is significant) and is not displayed for clarity reasons. FYROM corresponds to Former Yugoslav Republic of Macedonia.

* Data for Colombia and El Salvador refer to the urban population only.

** Estimations for Montenegro, Togo and Viet Nam do not account for sampling weights as they are missing in the data.

Source: Own calculations based on School-to-Work Transition Surveys 2012-2015, ILO.

Job security stands out clearly as an important driver of job satisfaction, whatever the employment status. As expected, young workers who are uncertain to keep their jobs have a much lower probability of being satisfied with their jobs (Figure 2.5, Panel A). The correlation is strong and significant in almost all countries and for all subpopulations considered. The effect is also of similar magnitude in urban and rural areas, across gender and across different types of employment (wage employment, self-employment and unpaid family work). In the same vein, wage employees benefiting from a contract of unlimited duration and from a written agreement are more likely to be satisfied with their jobs compared to those having a limited-duration contract or an oral agreement, respectively (Figure 2.5, Panel B).

Figure 2.5. Job security increases the likelihood of being satisfied at work

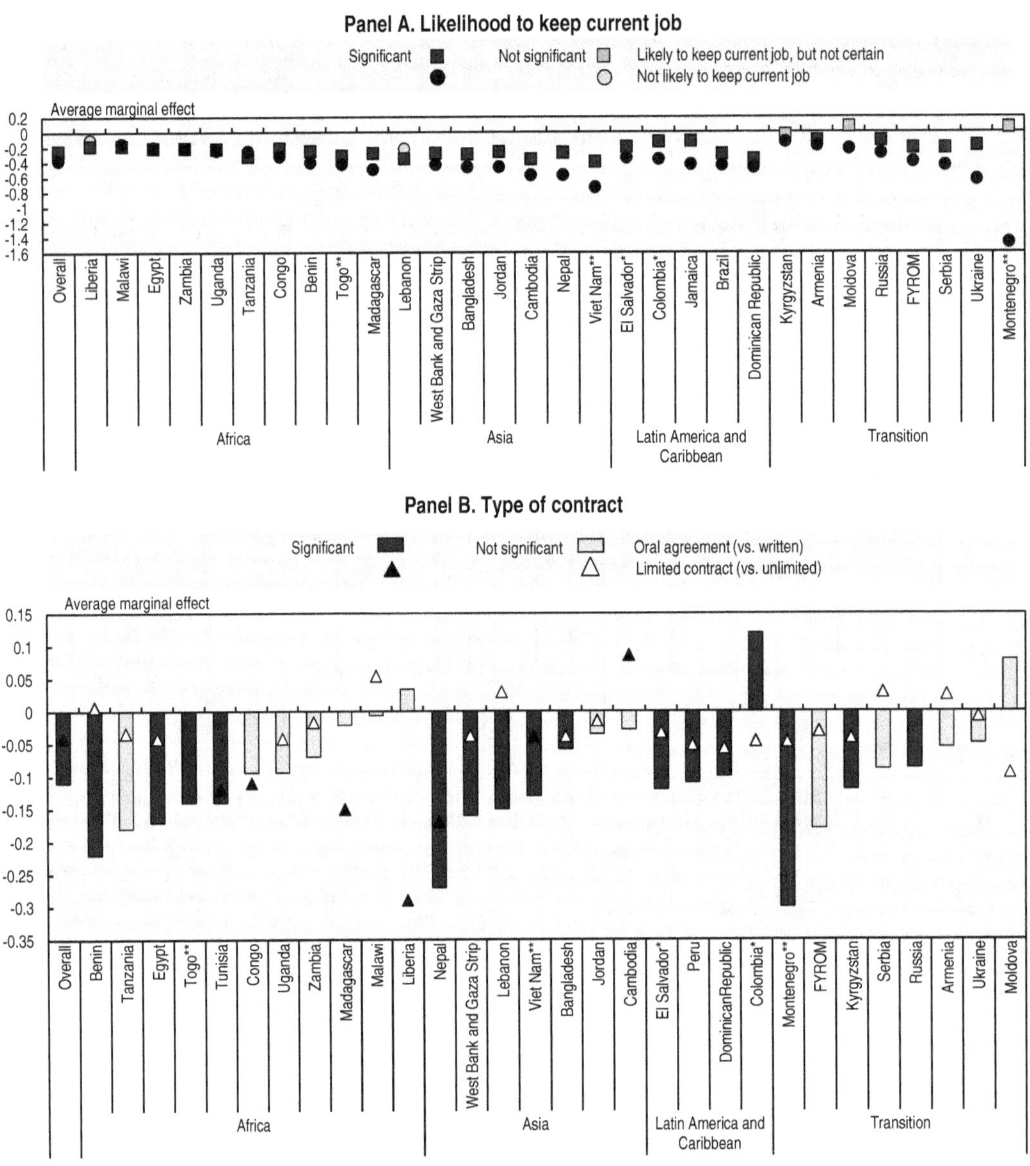

Note: The figure displays the average marginal effect of the likelihood of keeping the current job in comparison to being very likely to keep the job (Panel A), and of the type of contract for wage employees (Panel B), on the probability of being satisfied with the job (adjusted measure). The figure reads as follows: Being a wage employee benefiting from an oral agreement in Tunisia is associated with a decrease of 0.14 of the probability of being satisfied with the current job (adjusted measure) in comparison to being covered by a written agreement the Probit model described in Annex 2.A2 and displayed in Tables 2.A2.1, 2.A2.2 and 2.A2.3. Estimated associations that are significantly different from 0 (at the 95% confidence level) are represented in a darker tone. Estimations from Jamaica (Panel B), Peru (Panels A and B) and Tunisia (Panel A) are missing due to lack of data. FYROM corresponds to Former Yugoslav Republic of Macedonia.

* Data for Colombia and El Salvador refer to the urban population only.

** Estimations for Montenegro, Togo and Viet Nam do not account for sampling weights as they are missing in the data.

Source: Own calculations based on School-to-Work Transition Surveys 2012-2015, ILO.

Earnings exert only a small effect on young workers' satisfaction at work. Overall, standardised monthly income is positively and significantly associated with job satisfaction. However, the effect is somewhat small, as a large shift in monthly income (1 standard deviation) is associated with a relatively small change in the probability of being satisfied in comparison to other determinants (Figure 2.6). The link is valid for male and female workers alike, but the correlation is smaller and not significant for youth in rural areas.[3]

Figure 2.6. **Overall job satisfaction increases with earnings**

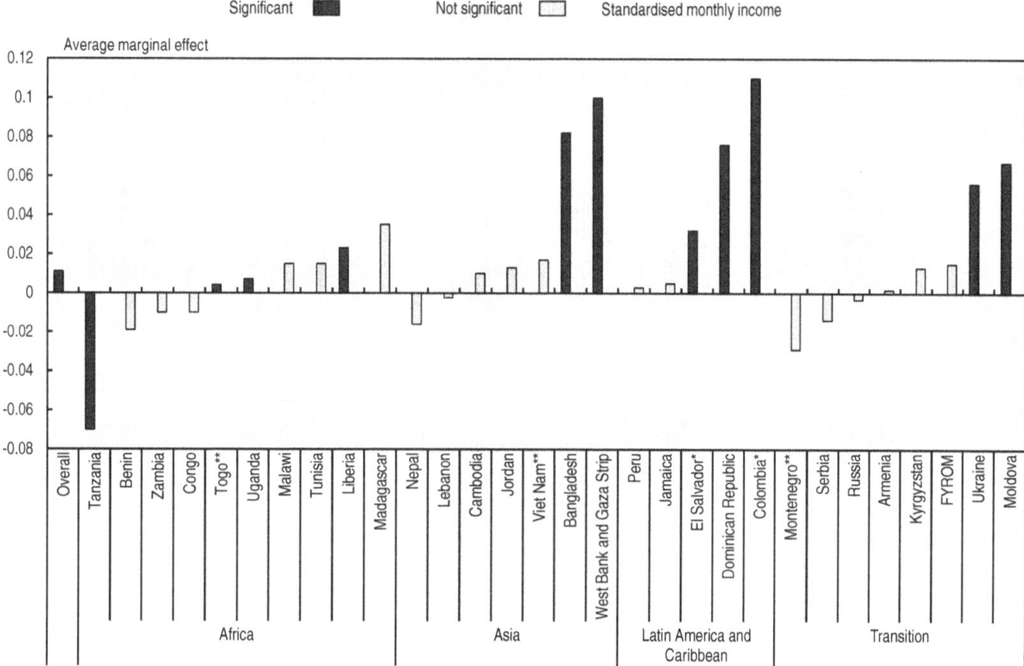

Note: The figure displays the average marginal effect of standardised monthly income on the probability of being satisfied with the job (adjusted measure). The figure reads as follows: an increase of 1 unit (corresponding here to 1 standard deviation) in monthly income in Madagascar is associated with an increase of 0.035 of the probability of being satisfied with the current job (adjusted measure) which is not statistically significant. The average marginal effects are estimated from the Probit model described in Annex 2.A2 and displayed in Tables 2.A2.1, 2.A2.2 and 2.A2.3. Estimated associations that are significantly different from 0 (at the 95% confidence level) are represented in a darker tone. Estimations from Jamaica (Panel B), Peru (Panels A and B) and Tunisia (Panel A) are missing due to lack of data. FYROM corresponds to Former Yugoslav Republic of Macedonia.

* Data for Colombia and El Salvador refer to the urban population only.

** Estimations for Montenegro, Togo and Viet Nam do not account for sampling weights as they are missing in the data.

Source: Own calculations based on School-to-Work Transition Surveys 2012-2015, ILO.

Skills mismatch is a strong driver of dissatisfaction at work, and all the more so when individuals are overqualified. Having relevant qualifications for a job, based on self-reporting measures, is significantly more satisfying for young workers than being underqualified or overqualified (Figure 2.7). This subjective measure of skills mismatch is referred to as over- or under-skilling, and is perceived as an accurate measure of skills mismatch amongst workers (McGuinness, Pouliakas and Redmond, 2017). More precisely, each young worker was asked: "Do you feel your education/training qualifications are relevant in performing your present job?" and could choose between the following three options: "Yes, they are relevant", "No, I feel overqualified" and "No, I feel underqualified". The results also clearly indicate that feeling overqualified appears to be much more detrimental to satisfaction than feeling underqualified. This result is very consistent across regions and countries. Interestingly, the perception of young workers of their skills adequacy affects wage employees, self-employed and unpaid family workers in a comparable way. The correlation decreases slightly for self-employed and unpaid family workers, but feeling overqualified remains more detrimental than feeling underqualified.

The correlation and order of magnitude does not vary across area of residence or gender. In the same vein, working in a firm that provides training opportunities is significantly correlated with a higher level of job satisfaction overall.

Figure 2.7. **Skills mismatch substantially reduces job satisfaction**

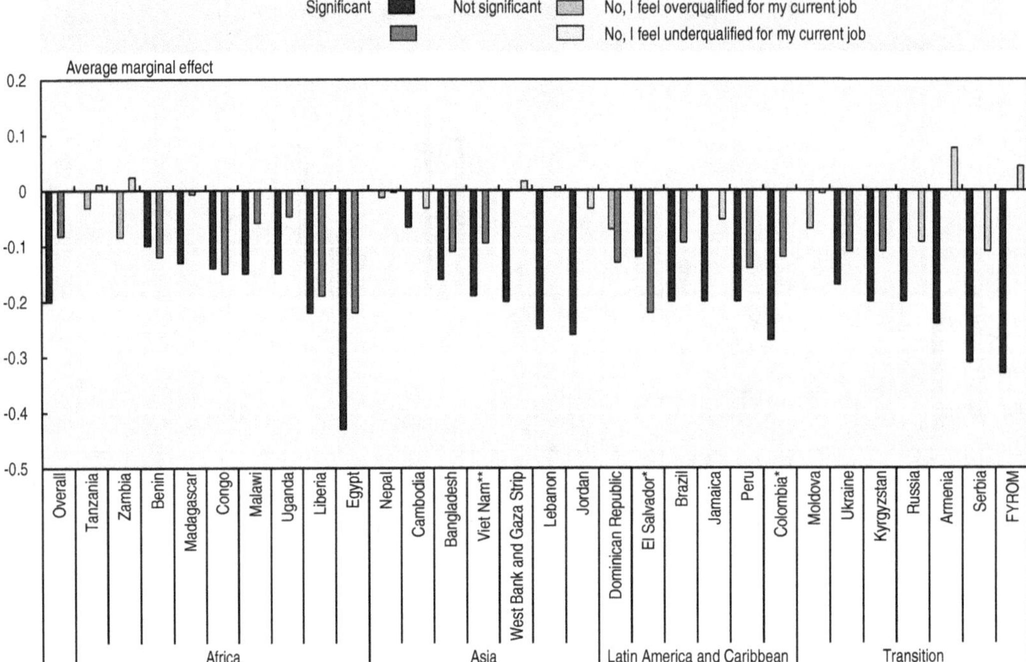

Note: The figure displays the average marginal effect of skills mismatch status on job satisfaction (adjusted measure) in comparison to having relevant skills for the current job. The respondent was asked: "Do you feel your education/training qualifications are relevant in performing your present job?" The figure reads as follows: Feeling overqualified in Malawi is associated with a decrease of 0.15 of the probability of being satisfied with the current job (adjusted measure) in comparison with feeling adequately trained. The average marginal effects are estimated from the Probit model described in Annex 2.A2 and displayed in Tables 2.A2.1, 2.A2.2 and 2.A2.3. Estimated associations that are significantly different from 0 (at the 95% confidence level) are represented in a darker tone. Estimations from Togo and Tunisia are missing due to lack of data. The coefficient associated with feeling overqualified in Montenegro is 0.8 and significantly different from zero. It is not represented for the clarity reasons.

* Data for Colombia and El Salvador refer to the urban population only. FYROM corresponds to Former Yugoslav Republic of Macedonia.

** Estimations for Montenegro, Togo and Viet Nam do not account for sampling weights as they are missing in the data.

Source: Own calculations based on School-to-Work Transition Surveys 2012-2015, ILO.

Notes

1. This statistical analysis relies on subjective well-being measures on a selected population of 15-29-year-old workers. As such, it is subject to different potential sources of bias and requires careful interpretation of the results. Some features of subjective well-being measures, such as hedonic adaptation and social comparisons, constitute well-known challenges to the interpretation of the results (Kahneman and Krueger, 2006). Moreover, the analysis focuses exclusively on young workers' assessment of job quality, which could be subject to some bias if the process guiding selection into employment is also correlated to the people's job satisfaction regardless of the intrinsic quality of the job. For example, in a high unemployment context, a young worker might be more likely to declare a higher level of job satisfaction simply out of relief at having a job. Conversely, 15-29-year-old people engaged in a professional activity are probably less qualified on average than those who are still studying, which in turn could translate into lower quality jobs and satisfaction. These limitations are inherent to engaging in a subjective well-being approach to youth employment quality and might affect the comparability of results across countries. They should be kept in mind when interpreting the results.

2. This section presents the results from a Probit regression of the adjusted measure of satisfaction on a set of individual and job characteristics (job facets) for each country, when all countries are pooled together. The statistical analysis provides correlation (and not causal effects) and, more precisely, the coefficients correspond to the average marginal effect of each variable. As such, the relative importance of each job facet for satisfaction can be assessed based on the magnitude of the estimated average marginal effect. However, the economic effect or relevance of each job facet should also be interpreted in light of its extent in the population.

3. Monthly income is not always well documented in the SWTS data, therefore caution is needed about the validity of this conclusion across countries.

References

Angner, E. (2012), "Subjective well-being: When, and why, it matters", *Working Paper*, University of Stockholm, https://papers.ssrn.com/sol3/papers.cfm?abstract_id=2157140.

Binder, M. (2014), "Subjective well-being capabilities: Bridging the gap between the capability approach and subjective well-being research", *Journal of Happiness Studies*, Vol. 15/ 5, 1197-1217, https://link.springer.com/article/10.1007/s10902-013-9471-6.

Blanchflower, D. and A. Oswald (2002), "Well-being over time in Britain and the USA", *Journal of Public Economics*, Vol. 88, pp. 1359-1386, https://link.springer.com/journal/10902.

Card, D., A. Mas, E. Moretti and E. Saez (2012), "Inequality at work: The effect of peer salaries on job satisfaction", *The American Economic Review*, Vol. 102/6, pp. 2981-3003. http://dx.doi.org/10.1257/aer.102.6.2981.

Clark, A. (2010), "Work, jobs, and well-being across the millennium", in Diener, E., D. Kahneman and J. Helliwell (eds.), *International Differences in Well-Being*, Oxford University Press, Oxford.

Deaton, A. and D. Kahneman (2010), "High income improves evaluation of life but not emotional well-being", *Proceedings of the National Academy of Sciences*, Vol. 107/38, http://www.pnas.org/content/107/38/16489.full.pdf.

Dolan, P., T. Peasgood and M. White (2008), "Do we really know what makes us happy? A review of the economic literature on the factors associated with subjective well-being", *Journal of Economic Psychology*, Vol. 29, pp. 94-122, https://doi.org/10.1016/j.joep.2007.09.001.

Eurofound (2012), *Trends in Job Quality in Europe*, Publications Office of the European Union, Luxembourg, https://www.eurofound.europa.eu/sites/default/files/ef_publication/field_ef_document/ef1228en_0.pdf.

Falco, P. and L. Haywood (2013), "Entrepreneurship vs. joblessness: Explaining the rise in self-employment", *Discussion Papers of DIW Berlin*, No. 1334, DIW Berlin, German Institute for Economic Research, https://www.diw.de/documents/publikationen/73/diw_01.c.430789.de/dp1334.pdf.

Ferrer-i-Carbonell, A. and X. Ramos (2010), "Inequality aversion and risk attitudes", *IZA Discussion Paper* N°4703, Institute for the Study of Labor (IZA), Bonn, http://ftp.iza.org/dp4703.pdf.

Gao, W. and R. Smyth (2010). "Job satisfaction and relative income in economic transition: Status or signal? The case of urban China", *China Economic Review*, Vol. 21, pp. 442-455, https://doi.org/10.1016/j.chieco.2010.04.002.

Green, F. (2011), "Unpacking the misery multiplier: How employability modifies the impacts of unemployment and job insecurity on life satisfaction and mental health", *Journal of Health Economics*, Vol. 30/2, pp. 265-276, https://doi.org/10.1016/j.jhealeco.2010.12.005.

Hijzen, A. and B. Menyhert (2016), "Measuring labour market security and assessing its implications for individual well-being", OECD *Social, Employment and Migration Working Papers*, No. 175, OECD Publishing, Paris, http://dx.doi.org/10.1787/5jm58qvzd6s4-en.

ILO (2015), *School-to-Work Transition Surveys*, International Labour Organization, Geneva, www.ilo.org/employment/areas/youth-employment/work-for-youth/WCMS_191853/lang--en/index.html.

ILO (2008), "Measuring decent work: tripartite meeting of experts on measurement of decent work", 8-10 Sept. 2008 (TMEMDW/2008) / International Labour Office. – Geneva, www.ilo.org/wcmsp5/groups/public/---dgreports/---integration/documents/meetingdocument/wcms_098027.pdf.

Kahneman, D. and A. B. Krueger (2006), "Developments in the measurement of subjective well-being", *The Journal of Economic Perspectives*, Vol. 20/1, pp. 3-24, http://dx.doi.org/10.1257/089533006776526030.

Kerber K.W. and J.P. Campbell (1987), "Job satisfaction: Identifying the important parts among computer sales and service personnel", *Journal of Business and Psychology*, Vol. 1/4, pp. 337-352, www.jstor.org/stable/25092109.

Knight, J. and R. Gunatilaka (2010a), "Great expectations? The subjective well-being of rural–urban migrants in China", *World Development*, Vol. 38, pp. 113-124, https://doi.org/10.1016/j.worlddev.2009.03.002

Knight, J., and R. Gunatilaka (2010b), "The rural-urban divide in China: Income but not happiness?" *Journal of Development Studies*, Vol. 46, 506-29, http://dx.doi.org/10.1080/00220380903012763.

Latif, E. (2010), "Crisis, unemployment and psychological wellbeing in Canada", *Journal of Policy Modeling*, Vol. 32, pp. 520-530, https://doi.org/10.1016/j.jpolmod.2010.05.010.

McGuinness S., K. Pouliakas and P. Redmond (2017), "How useful is the concept of skills mismatch?", *Skills and Employability Branch, Employment Policy Department*, International Labour Organization, Geneva, www.ilo.org/wcmsp5/groups/public/---ed_emp/---ifp_skills/documents/publication/wcms_552798.pdf.

McKee-Ryan, F., Z. Song, C. Wanberg and A. Kinicki (2005), "Psychological and physical well-being during unemployment: A meta-analytic study", *Journal of Applied Psychology*, Vol. 90, pp. 53-76, DOI: 10.1037/0021-9010.90.1.53.

Mueller, C.W. and S.W. Kim (2008), "The contented female worker: Still a paradox?", in Karen A. Hegtvedt, Jody Clay-Warner (ed.), *Justice* (Advances in Group Processes, Volume 25) Emerald Group Publishing Limited, pp.117 – 149, www.emeraldinsight.com/doi/pdfplus/10.1016/S0882-6145%2808%2925006-X.

Nikolova, M. (2016), "Happiness and development", IZA *Discussion Paper* N°10088, Institute for the Study of Labor (IZA), Bonn, http://ftp.iza.org/dp10088.pdf.

OECD (2017a), *Unlocking the Potential of Youth Entrepreneurship in Developing Countries: From Subsistence to Performance*, OECD Development Centre Studies, OECD Publishing, Paris, http://dx.doi.org/10.1787/9789264277830-en.

OECD (2017b), *OECD Guidelines on Measuring the Quality of the Working Environment*, OECD Publishing, Paris, http://dx.doi.org/10.1787/9789264278240-en.

OECD (2015), *OECD Employment Outlook 2015*, OECD Publishing, Paris, http://dx.doi.org/10.1787/empl_outlook-2015-en.

OECD (2014), *OECD Employment Outlook 2014*, OECD Publishing, Paris, http://dx.doi.org/10.1787/empl_outlook-2014-en.

OECD (2013), *How's Life? 2013: Measuring Well-being*, OECD Publishing, Paris, http://dx.doi.org/10.1787/9789264201392-en.

OECD (2012), *Sick on the Job?: Myths and Realities about Mental Health and Work, Mental Health and Work*, OECD Publishing, Paris, http://dx.doi.org/10.1787/9789264124523-en.

OECD (2011), "Earnings volatility: Causes and consequences", *OECD Employment Outlook 2011*, OECD Publishing, Paris, http://dx.doi.org/10.1787/empl_outlook-2011-5-en.

Ravallion M. and M. Lokshin (2010), "Who cares about relative deprivation?", *Journal of Economic Behavior and Organization*, Vol. 73, pp. 171-185, https://doi.org/10.1016/j.jebo.2009.08.008.

Sacks, D., B. Stevenson and J. Wolfers (2012), "The new stylized facts about income and subjective well-being", *Emotion*, Vol. 12/6, pp. 1181-1187, http://dx.doi.org/10.1037/a0029873.

Senik, C. (2009), "Income distribution and subjective happiness: A survey", *OECD Social Employment and Migration Working Papers*, No. 96, OECD Publishing, Paris, http://dx.doi.org/10.1787/218860720683.

Stevenson, B. and J. Wolfers (2013), "Subjective well-being and income: Is there any evidence of satiation?" *The American Economic Review*, Vol. 103/3, pp. 598-604, http://dx.doi.org/10.1257/aer.103.3.598.

Stevenson, B. and J. Wolfers (2008), "Economic growth and subjective well-being: Reassessing the Easterlin paradox", *Brookings Papers on Economic Activity, Economic Studies Program,* The Brookings Institution, vol. 39(1 (Spring), pages 1-102, http://dx.doi.org/10.3386/w14282

Stiglitz, J., A. Sen and J.P. Fitoussi (2009), "The measurement of economic performance and social progress revisited: Reflections and overview", *Document de travail de l'OFCE,* N°2009-33, http://spire.sciencespo.fr/hdl:/2441/5l6uh8ogmqildh09h4687h53k/resources/wp2009-33.pdf.

Theodossiou, I. (1998), "The effects of low-pay and unemployment on psychological well-being: A logistic regression approach", *Journal of Health Economics,* Vol. 17, pp. 85-104, https://doi.org/10.1016/S0167-6296(97)00018-0.

Annex 2.A1. Documentation on the adjusted measure of job satisfaction

This annex provides additional information and discusses the relationship between job satisfaction measured on a 1-to-4 scale and workers' desire to change jobs. Figure 2.A1.1 shows that workers who are either somewhat satisfied or very satisfied might still wish to change jobs, and that the proportion of satisfied workers who wish to change jobs is substantial and averages 28% across countries. Most young workers who express satisfaction with their jobs would like to change jobs in order to improve the quality of their employment situation (Figure 2.A1.2). This supports the methodological choice of assessing job satisfaction based on the combination of the two variables. Nevertheless, the higher the job satisfaction, the less likely are individuals to wish to change jobs and be actively looking for a job. This shows that, overall, young workers are consistent in judging their employment situations (Figure 2.A1.3).

Figure 2.A1.1. Share of young workers who are satisfied but still wish to change jobs (%)

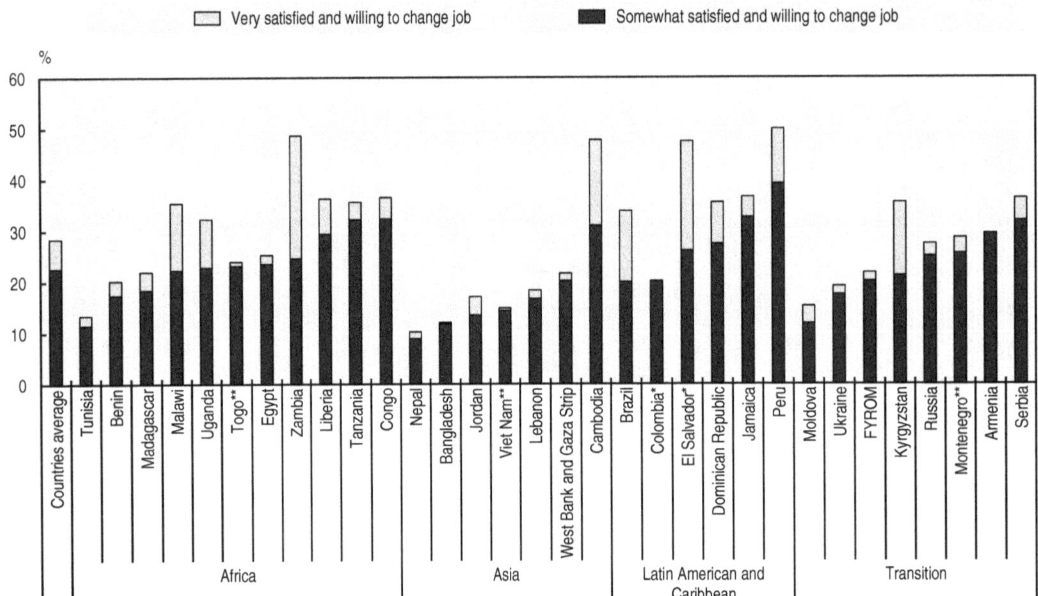

Note: Countries are sorted by the proportion of young workers who say they are somewhat satisfied and yet wish to change jobs within each group. FYROM corresponds to Former Yugoslav Republic of Macedonia.

* Data for Colombia and El Salvador refer to the urban population only.

** Estimations for Montenegro, Togo and Viet Nam do not account for sampling weights as they are missing in the data.

Source: Own calculations based on School-to-Work Transition Surveys 2012-2015, ILO.

Figure 2.A1.2. **Satisfied young workers wish to change jobs for various reasons**

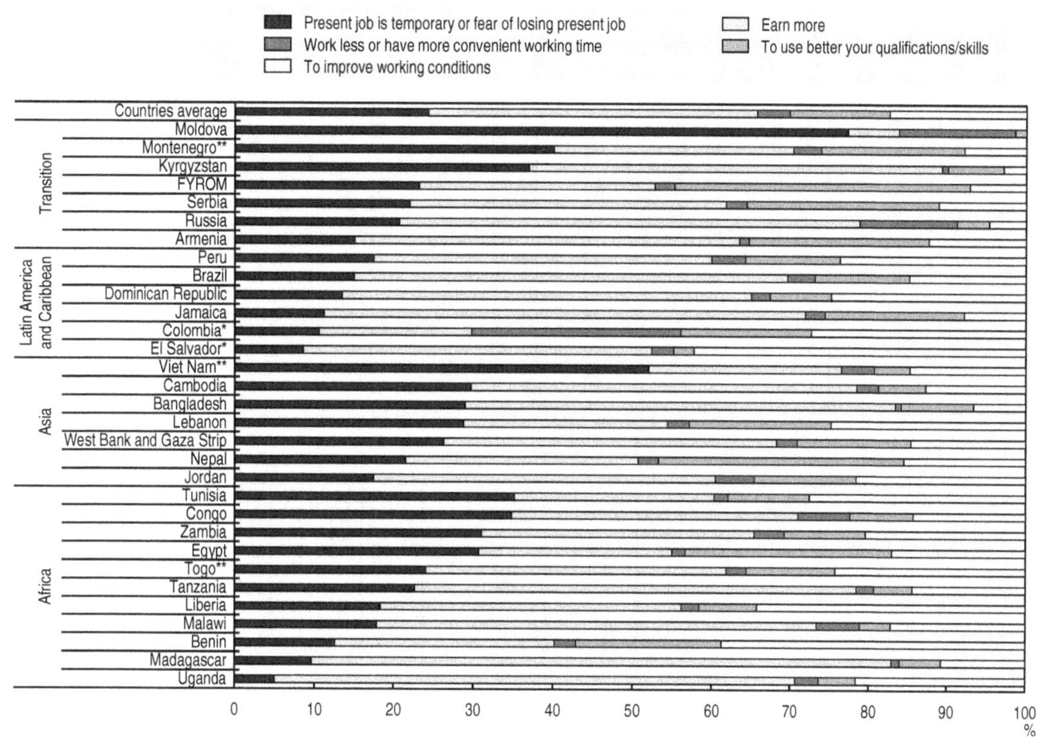

Note: Countries are sorted by the proportion of young workers wishing to change jobs because their present job is temporary or they fear losing it, within each group. FYROM corresponds to Former Yugoslav Republic of Macedonia.

* Data for Colombia and El Salvador refer to the urban population only.

** Estimations for Montenegro, Togo and Viet Nam do not account for sampling weights as they are missing in the data.

Source: Own calculations based on School-to-Work Transition Surveys 2012-2015, ILO.

Figure 2.A1.3. **Satisfied young workers are less likely to want to change jobs (Panel A) and to look actively for a new job (Panel B)**

Panel A. Wishing to change job

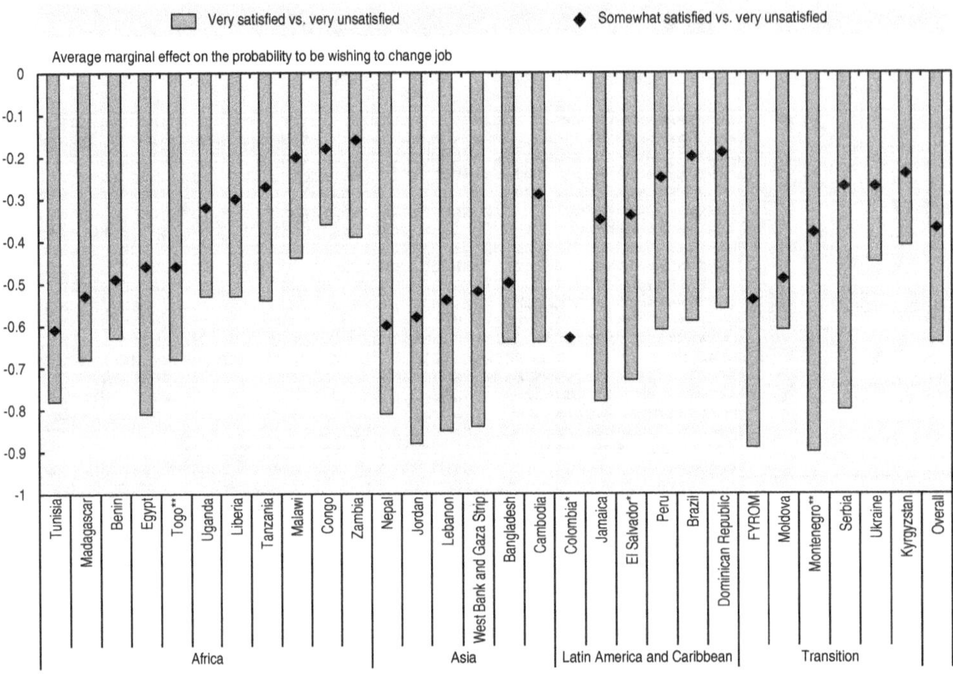

Panel B. Actively looking for another job

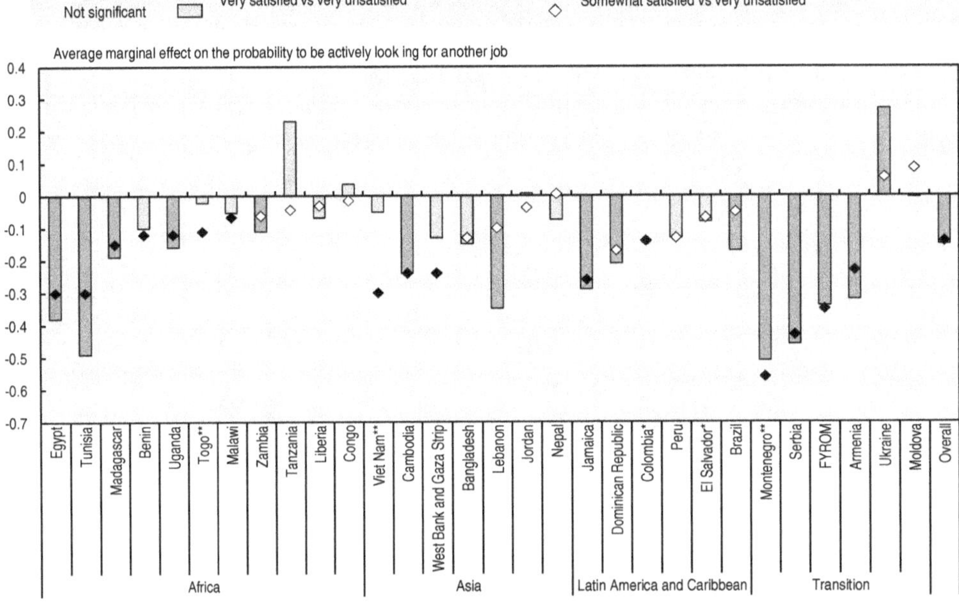

Note: The figure displays the average marginal effect of worker satisfaction level on the probability of wishing to change jobs (Panel A) and of actively looking for a job (Panel B). The figure reads as follows: Being very satisfied with one's job is associated with a decrease of 0.89 of the probability of wishing to change jobs in Moldova, in comparison to be very unsatisfied. The average marginal effects are estimated from the Probit model described in Annex 2.A2 and displayed in Tables 2.A2.1, 2.A2.2 and 2.A2.3. Estimated associations that are significantly different from 0 (at the 95% confidence level) are represented in a darker tone. Estimations from Viet Nam (Panel A) and Kyrgyzstan (Panel B) are missing due to lack of data. Estimates for Colombia are based on the comparison of two categories only, satisfied workers and unsatisfied workers, which is therefore the reference category for Colombia. FYROM corresponds to Former Yugoslav Republic of Macedonia.

* Data for Colombia and El Salvador refer to the urban population only.

** Estimations for Montenegro, Togo and Viet Nam do not account for sampling weights as they are missing in the data.

Source: Own calculations based on School-to-Work Transition Surveys 2012-2015, ILO.

Annex 2.A2. Statistical analysis of job satisfaction

This annex provides the overall findings from the statistical analysis of job satisfaction from which partial results have been selected and presented in figures in the core of the report. Tables 2.A2.1 to 2.A2.3 display the results from the main regression analysis at the country level. Table 2.A2.4 presents the results for a similar regression analysis on different subpopulations, namely female, male, urban and rural young workers. Table 2.A2.5 corresponds to a statistical analysis of job satisfaction specific to the different employment statuses, wage employees, self-employed workers and unpaid family workers. For reasons of clarity, the results from the same regression analysis are presented separately in Tables 2.A2.1, 2.A2.2 and 2.A2.3, which respectively refer to the impact of socio-economic and demographic characteristics, structural aspects of employment (employment status, occupation and industry) and other qualitative aspects of jobs.

All of the following tables display average marginal effects estimated from a Probit model with the adjusted measure of satisfaction (i.e. a dummy equal to 1 if a young worker is satisfied with his/her job and does not want to change jobs) as the dependent variable. Column headers indicate the subpopulation on which the analysis focuses, and explanatory variables are listed in rows. Due to the inclusion of standardised monthly income as an explanatory variable, the analysis de facto excludes unpaid family workers in Tables 2.A2.1 to 2.A2.4. By and large, the conclusions hold when monthly income is dropped from the analysis and unpaid family workers are accounted for.

Explanatory variables includes socio-economic characteristics of the worker (age, sex, area of residence, household financial status, level of education, father's education and occupation, health status); current job characteristics (sector and occupation categories, employment status, whether the activity is registered or not, and whether training is provided); and other indicators of job quality (such as how long the worker has looked for the job, whether she/he is also studying, considers herself/himself adequately trained for the job, and expects to keep working in the current activity over the next 12 months).In addition to the variables displayed in the tables, survey year and country fixed effects are also included as explanatory variables in the specifications where all countries are pulled together. Due to the absence of weights' variable for Montenegro, Togo and Viet Nam, the weights are never used in these specifications. For the statistical analysis at the country level, all available rounds of the SWTS are used, and survey year fixed effects are included as additional control variables when this applies. Statistically significant coefficients at the 99.9%, 99% and 95% confidence levels are respectively indicated by ***, ** and *. The number of observations is indicated by N.

Table 2.A2.1. Impact of the socio-economic characteristics of young workers on job satisfaction, overall and by country

		OVERALL (All 32 countries)	AFRICA										
			Benin	Congo	Egypt	Liberia	Madagascar	Malawi	Tanzania	Togo**	Tunisia	Uganda	Zambia
	Age (in years)	0.00014	0.0026	0.0061	0.0012	0.0050	0.0014	-0.0059*	-0.0025	-0.0083*	0.0037	-0.0056	-0.0054
		(0.00064)	(0.0038)	(0.0051)	(0.0020)	(0.0031)	(0.0039)	(0.0027)	(0.0065)	(0.0040)	(0.0045)	(0.0032)	(0.0045)
	Female (Ref. Male)	0.00041	-0.0062	0.056	0.074***	0.022	-0.049	0.0059	-0.041	0.067*	0.044	-0.014	0.022
		(0.0048)	(0.026)	(0.039)	(0.020)	(0.037)	(0.032)	(0.022)	(0.052)	(0.031)	(0.036)	(0.025)	(0.033)
	Rural (Ref. Urban)	0.0048	0.040	-0.045	0.052***	0.038	0.025	0.056*	0.018	-0.0035	-0.037	0.028	-0.12***
		(0.0054)	(0.030)	(0.045)	(0.015)	(0.042)	(0.036)	(0.028)	(0.054)	(0.035)	(0.034)	(0.028)	(0.031)
Household financial situation: Ref. Well-off	Fairly well-off	-0.021		-0.10	-0.032	0.16	0.019	-0.065	-0.40*	-0.28	0.095	-0.10	-0.26*
		(0.012)		(0.11)	(0.045)	(0.10)	(0.10)	(0.16)	(0.18)	(0.24)	(0.13)	(0.12)	(0.12)
	Average	-0.088***		-0.14	-0.10*	0.10	0.047	-0.047	-0.46*	-0.31	-0.14	-0.15	-0.26*
		(0.011)		(0.10)	(0.044)	(0.098)	(0.087)	(0.16)	(0.18)	(0.24)	(0.11)	(0.11)	(0.12)
	Fairly poor	-0.15***		-0.21*	-0.13**	0.051	-0.071	-0.12	-0.48**	-0.40	-0.20	-0.18	-0.29*
		(0.012)		(0.11)	(0.047)	(0.098)	(0.088)	(0.15)	(0.18)	(0.23)	(0.12)	(0.11)	(0.12)
	Very poor	-0.20***		-0.26*	-0.27***	0.057	-0.095	-0.20	-0.66***	-0.44	-0.28*	-0.21	-0.25*
		(0.013)		(0.11)	(0.064)	(0.100)	(0.084)	(0.15)	(0.18)	(0.24)	(0.13)	(0.12)	(0.12)
Father's education completed: Ref. No schooling	Primary	-0.011	0.054	0.047	-0.0077	0.016	-0.0043	-0.049	-0.13	-0.035	0.084*	-0.011	-0.13
		(0.0069)	(0.046)	(0.055)	(0.023)	(0.046)	(0.045)	(0.025)	(0.082)	(0.037)	(0.039)	(0.027)	(0.083)
	Secondary general	-0.023**	0.044	-0.016	0.016	-0.019	-0.065	-0.0022	-0.12	-0.081*	0.033	-0.0014	-0.13
		(0.0084)	(0.056)	(0.055)	(0.080)	(0.044)	(0.058)	(0.038)	(0.095)	(0.041)	(0.049)	(0.080)	(0.082)
	Vocational studies	-0.038***	0.083	0.055	-0.022	0.13	0.066	-0.024	0.12	-0.026	-0.033	0.0087	-0.16
		(0.010)	(0.16)	(0.075)	(0.023)	(0.086)	(0.17)	(0.060)	(0.16)	(0.088)	(0.14)	(0.065)	(0.084)
	Tertiary	-0.011	0.14	-0.055	0.00039	-0.064	0.14	0.038	-0.24*	-0.15	0.11	0.0046	-0.15
		(0.011)	(0.096)	(0.071)	(0.031)	(0.073)	(0.11)	(0.039)	(0.11)	(0.12)	(0.085)	(0.099)	(0.097)
Young workers' completed education: Ref. No schooling	Primary	-0.031***		0.077	-0.0096	-0.021	0.039	-0.025	-0.12	-0.13	0.11	-0.071**	0.16***
		(0.0090)		(0.054)	(0.024)	(0.055)	(0.10)	(0.026)	(0.18)	(0.081)	(0.11)	(0.026)	(0.029)
	Secondary vocational	-0.054***		0.029	-0.027	0.20	-0.053	-0.11	-0.22	-0.17	0.15	0.061	0.17***
		(0.013)		(0.078)	(0.026)	(0.14)	(0.16)	(0.095)	(0.19)	(0.12)	(0.11)	(0.076)	(0.035)
	Secondary general	-0.061***		0.071	-0.11	-0.13*	-0.029	-0.11**	-0.21	-0.16	0.10	-0.14	0.22***
		(0.0098)		(0.055)	(0.073)	(0.058)	(0.11)	(0.038)	(0.18)	(0.086)	(0.11)	(0.074)	(0.027)
	Post-secondary vocational	-0.082***		0.085	0.0059	-0.036		0.041	-0.25	-0.23		0.056	0.28***
		(0.013)	(0.23)	(0.15)	(0.070)	(0.10)		(0.16)	(0.083)	(0.051)		(0.053)	
	Graduate	-0.087***	-0.46*	-0.10	-0.047	-0.052	-0.20***	-0.047	0.017	-0.055	0.090	0.21**	
		(0.012)	(0.20)	(0.067)	(0.062)	(0.045)	(0.047)	(0.14)	(0.065)	(0.051)	(0.12)	(0.079)	
	Post-graduate	-0.11***			-0.050		-0.42***		0.045	-0.079	0.18		
		(0.022)			(0.10)		(0.094)		(0.17)	(0.11)	(0.12)		
Ref. No health issues	At least one health issue	-0.049***	-0.050	-0.12**	-0.079*	-0.011	-0.011	-0.061	-0.017		0.17***	0.0077	
		(0.0079)	(0.059)	(0.041)	(0.039)	(0.030)	(0.12)	(0.034)	(0.038)		(0.051)	(0.039)	
	N	37888	1386	853	3917	1081	2105	2522	521	1104	691	1581	1171

Note: The table displays average marginal effects estimated from a Probit model with the adjusted measure of satisfaction (i.e. a dummy equal to 1 if a young worker is satisfied with his/her job and does not want to change jobs) as the dependent variable. Column headers indicate the subpopulation on which the analysis focuses, and explanatory variables are listed in rows. This table presents only the results from a subset of all explanatory variables used in the regression analysis. The results relating to the other explanatory variables are provided in Table 2.A2.2 and Table 2.A2.3. Due to the inclusion of standardised monthly income as an explanatory variable, the analysis de facto excludes unpaid family workers. By and large, the conclusions hold when monthly income is dropped from the analysis and unpaid family workers are accounted for. In addition to the variables displayed in the tables, survey year and country fixed effects are also included as explanatory variables in the specifications where all countries are pulled together (corresponding to the column header "Overall"). Estimations for Montenegro, Togo and Viet Nam do not account for sampling weights as they are missing in the data. The analysis for Colombia and El Salvador refer to the urban population only. For the statistical analysis at the country level, all available rounds of the SWTS are used, and survey year fixed effects are included as additional control variables when this applies. Statistically significant coefficients at the 99.9%, 99% and 95% confidence levels are respectively indicated by ***, ** and *. The number of observations is indicated by N.
Source: Own calculations based on School-to-Work Transition Surveys 2012-2015, ILO.

Table 2.A2.1. Impact of the socio-economic characteristics of young workers on job satisfaction, overall and by country (cont.)

		Bangladesh	Cambodia	Jordan	Lebanon	Nepal	Viet Nam**	West Bank and Gaza Strip
	Age (in years)	-0.00018	-0.0044	0.00028	0.0046	-0.0057	0.0014	0.0016
		(0.0029)	(0.0025)	(0.0035)	(0.0049)	(0.0060)	(0.0024)	(0.0039)
	Female (Ref. Male)	0.080**	0.011	0.023	-0.018	-0.0091	-0.017	0.068
		(0.030)	(0.019)	(0.038)	(0.036)	(0.045)	(0.016)	(0.041)
	Rural (Ref. Urban)	-0.065*	0.027	-0.0049	0.056	-0.073		-0.039
		(0.025)	(0.025)	(0.023)	(0.035)	(0.052)		(0.031)
Household financial situation: Ref. Well-off	Fairly well-off	-0.079*		-0.045	0.011		-0.053	-0.12**
		(0.039)		(0.031)	(0.043)		(0.079)	(0.038)
	Average	-0.11*		-0.075*	-0.066		-0.086	-0.16***
		(0.043)		(0.033)	(0.043)		(0.073)	(0.043)
	Fairly poor	-0.17***		-0.083*	-0.036		-0.12	-0.22**
		(0.044)		(0.041)	(0.065)		(0.077)	(0.071)
	Very poor			-0.0090	-0.089		-0.17*	-0.34**
				(0.074)	(0.13)		(0.080)	(0.11)
Father's education completed: Ref. No schooling	Primary	-0.0030	-0.0013	-0.055*		0.051	0.012	0.028
		(0.028)	(0.024)	(0.027)		(0.048)	(0.024)	(0.033)
	Secondary general	-0.18	0.052	-0.12**		-0.010	-0.037	-0.013
		(0.12)	(0.032)	(0.044)		(0.071)	(0.034)	(0.044)
	Vocational studies	-0.21	0.036	-0.11		-0.063	-0.026	0.11
		(0.23)	(0.061)	(0.060)		(0.12)	(0.025)	(0.059)
	Tertiary	0.024	0.13	-0.020		-0.0029	-0.017	0.030
		(0.078)	(0.11)	(0.038)		(0.13)	(0.048)	(0.053)
Young workers' completed education: Ref. No schooling	Primary	-0.039	-0.024	-0.0043	0.071		-0.017	-0.11**
		(0.025)	(0.040)	(0.052)	(0.17)		(0.036)	(0.037)
	Secondary vocational		0.0025	-0.034	0.096		-0.044	-0.086
			(0.068)	(0.071)	(0.18)		(0.036)	(0.073)
	Secondary general	-0.13*	-0.057	-0.037	0.16		-0.0016	-0.0084
		(0.060)	(0.043)	(0.063)	(0.18)		(0.039)	(0.039)
	Post-secondary vocational	-0.17	0.0034	-0.059	0.046		-0.094	-0.16**
		(0.18)	(0.19)		(0.19)			(0.19)
	Graduate	-0.24**	-0.072	-0.037	0.039			-0.046
		(0.086)	(0.19)	(0.15)	(0.18)			(0.19)
	Post-graduate	-0.39***	0.13		0.16			-0.051
		(0.10)	(0.33)		(0.19)			(0.19)
Ref. No health issues	At least one health issue	-0.026		-0.080		-0.070		-0.042
		(0.064)		(0.041)		(0.066)		(0.032)
	N	1933	2608	2440	639	552	2110	1462

Table 2.A2.1. **Impact of the socio-economic characteristics of young workers on job satisfaction, overall and by country** (cont.)

		LATIN AMERICA AND CARIBBEAN					
		Brazil	Colombia*	Dominican Republic	El Salvador*	Jamaica	Peru
	Age (in years)	0.0017	-0.0072*	0.0084	-0.00045	0.0078	-0.0067
		(0.0029)	(0.0033)	(0.0051)	(0.0041)	(0.0050)	(0.0057)
	Female (Ref. Male)	-0.021	0.010	0.071	0.032	0.066	-0.084
		(0.025)	(0.025)	(0.043)	(0.038)	(0.040)	(0.043)
	Rural (Ref. Urban)	0.073*		0.0018		-0.0057	-0.0032
		(0.033)		(0.035)		(0.035)	(0.044)
Household financial situation: Ref. Well-off	Fairly well-off	-0.072	-0.076	-0.26	-0.022	-0.12	0.12
		(0.046)	(0.068)	(0.14)	(0.13)	(0.13)	(0.19)
	Average	-0.16***	-0.21**	-0.32***	-0.028	-0.092	-0.0035
		(0.047)	(0.071)	(0.067)	(0.085)	(0.12)	(0.19)
	Fairly poor	-0.32***	-0.30*	-0.40***	-0.15	-0.21	-0.091
		(0.058)	(0.13)	(0.066)	(0.089)	(0.12)	(0.20)
	Very poor		-0.67***	-0.42***	-0.18*	-0.14	-0.19
			(0.069)	(0.079)	(0.086)	(0.12)	(0.22)
Father's education completed: Ref. No schooling	Primary		0.034	0.033	0.12**	0.11	-0.075
			(0.032)	(0.044)	(0.038)	(0.16)	(0.075)
	Secondary general		0.025	0.016	0.086	0.090	-0.080
			(0.036)	(0.058)	(0.071)	(0.16)	(0.072)
	Vocational studies		0.046	-0.21	0.57*	0.059	-0.20*
			(0.057)	(0.13)	(0.24)	(0.17)	(0.094)
	Tertiary		-0.054	0.062	0.034	0.17	-0.088
			(0.060)	(0.15)	(0.13)	(0.18)	(0.10)
Young worker's completed education : Ref. no schooling	Primary		0.11	0.037	-0.39*	0.023	0.18
			(0.28)	(0.074)	(0.18)	(0.19)	(0.16)
	Secondary vocational			0.23*		-0.040	
				(0.12)		(0.21)	
	Secondary general		0.11	0.012	-0.44*	0.043	0.046
			(0.28)	(0.073)	(0.19)	(0.19)	(0.16)
	Post-secondary vocational		0.12	0.0015	-0.45*	0.0064	-0.035
			(0.28)	(0.13)	(0.11)		(0.16)
	Graduate		0.043	-0.13	-0.14	-0.11	0.0029
			(0.28)	(0.10)	(0.11)	(0.17)	(0.17)
	Post-graduate		0.045			-0.19	
			(0.30)			(0.19)	
Ref. No health issues	At least one health issue			0.073	-0.15***	-0.022	-0.22
				(0.063)	(0.038)	(0.059)	(0.16)
	N	1626	3128	973	1956	908	670

Table 2.A2.1. **Impact of the socio-economic characteristics of young workers on job satisfaction, overall and by country** (cont.)

		TRANSITION						
	Armenia	Kyrgyzstan	Former Yugoslav Republic of Macedonia	Moldova	Montenegro**	Russia	Serbia	Ukraine
Age (in years)	-0.00093	0.0034	0.0036	-0.011	-0.015	0.0078	-0.0074	0.0056
	(0.0061)	(0.0054)	(0.0066)	(0.0068)	(0.035)	(0.0061)	(0.0069)	(0.0042)
Female (Ref. Male)	0.011	0.042	0.037	0.031	0.017	-0.00058	0.067	-0.027
	(0.034)	(0.038)	(0.034)	(0.042)	(0.23)	(0.040)	(0.043)	(0.023)
Rural (Ref. Urban)	-0.052	0.016	0.059	0.028	0.13	0.050	0.11**	0.042
	(0.037)	(0.037)	(0.035)	(0.044)	(0.20)	(0.039)	(0.041)	(0.026)
Household financial situation: Ref. Well-off								
Fairly well-off	-0.056	0.22***	-0.027	0.10	0.11	-0.031	0.23*	0.034
	(0.073)	(0.060)	(0.048)	(0.091)	(0.42)	(0.065)	(0.091)	(0.20)
Average	-0.100	0.19***	-0.049	-0.0084	0.18	-0.16**	-0.096	0.046
	(0.067)	(0.051)	(0.051)	(0.058)	(0.32)	(0.060)	(0.075)	(0.19)
Fairly poor	-0.099	0.012	-0.16**	-0.13	0.39	-0.35***	-0.18*	-0.043
	(0.074)	(0.086)	(0.055)	(0.083)	(0.46)	(0.071)	(0.086)	(0.19)
Very poor	-0.16	0.15	-0.23***	-0.25	-0.41	-0.27*	-0.25**	-0.13
	(0.092)	(0.23)	(0.061)	(0.15)	(0.44)	(0.12)	(0.091)	(0.19)
Father's education completed: Ref. No schooling								
Primary		-0.34***	0.20		-0.077		0.16	
		(0.096)	(0.13)		(0.79)		(0.12)	
Secondary general	0.38*	-0.31***	0.045	0.26**	0.35		0.18	
	(0.16)	(0.070)	(0.14)	(0.083)	(1.02)		(0.11)	
Vocational studies	0.36*	-0.40***	0.15	0.19*	0.023		0.077	
	(0.16)	(0.074)	(0.13)	(0.080)	(0.74)		(0.13)	
Tertiary	0.35*	-0.27***	0.089	0.18	0.77		0.24*	
	(0.16)	(0.079)	(0.15)	(0.092)	(0.81)		(0.12)	
Young workers' completed education: Ref. No schooling								
Primary		0.099	-0.055		2.85**	-0.027	-0.63***	
		(0.21)	(0.17)		(0.88)	(0.21)	(0.075)	
Secondary vocational		0.22	-0.0013		1.09	-0.14	-0.23*	0.053
		(0.21)	(0.16)		(0.65)	(0.21)	(0.10)	(0.19)
Secondary general		0.23	-0.026		0.70	-0.15	-0.46***	0.026
		(0.20)	(0.16)		(0.90)	(0.21)	(0.057)	(0.19)
Post-secondary vocational		0.26			2.47**	-0.17	-0.089	0.025
	(0.044)	(0.21)		(0.10)	(0.90)			
Graduate	-0.11**	0.15		-0.055	1.27*			
	(0.036)	(0.21)		(0.11)	(0.62)			
Post-graduate	-0.059							
	(0.099)							
Ref. No health issues								
At least one health issue	-0.027	-0.12		-0.0076	-0.13	0.015	-0.11**	
	(0.027)	(0.074)		(0.029)	(0.77)	(0.055)	(0.040)	
N	1048	1039	675	404	258	860	566	1688

Table 2.A2.2. Impact of employment status, occupation and industry on job satisfaction, overall and by country

		OVERALL (All 32 countries)	AFRICA										
			Benin	Congo	Egypt	Liberia	Madagascar	Malawi	Tanzania	Togo**	Tunisia	Uganda	Zambia
	Self-employed (Ref. Wage employee)	0.066***	0.19***	0.021	0.057*	0.057	-0.15**	0.074**	0.031	0.27***	0.078	0.16***	0.16***
		(0.0071)	(0.053)	(0.051)	(0.025)	(0.064)	(0.047)	(0.029)	(0.056)	(0.060)	(0.067)	(0.033)	(0.035)
Occupation: Ref. High skilled (ISCO 1-3)	Medium skilled / Services (ISCO 4-5)	-0.026**	-0.026	-0.037	-0.13***	0.20*	-0.100	0.010	-0.23	0.073		0.042	-0.031
		(0.0082)	(0.049)	(0.087)	(0.027)	(0.083)	(0.091)	(0.058)	(0.13)	(0.084)		(0.069)	(0.047)
	Medium skilled / Agriculture (ISCO 6)	-0.036**	0.0097	-0.020	-0.16*	0.016	-0.052	0.050	-0.061	0.26*		-0.076	0.019
		(0.013)	(0.054)	(0.12)	(0.065)	(0.090)	(0.10)	(0.067)	(0.16)	(0.11)		(0.086)	(0.099)
	Medium skilled / Manufacturing (ISCO 7-8)	-0.026**	-0.031	-0.089	-0.072*	0.17	-0.15	-0.0093	-0.18	0.22*		0.024	0.070
		(0.0094)	(0.056)	(0.093)	(0.028)	(0.095)	(0.11)	(0.066)	(0.13)	(0.090)		(0.075)	(0.066)
	Low skilled (ISCO 9)	-0.081***	-0.13*	-0.24*	-0.15***	0.15	-0.13	-0.046	-0.21	0.16		-0.072	0.014
		(0.010)	(0.064)	(0.10)	(0.036)	(0.086)	(0.089)	(0.063)	(0.13)	(0.10)		(0.080)	(0.058)
Industry: ref. Agriculture and fishery (ISIC 1)	Manufacturing, mining, etc. (ISIC 2-6)	0.043***	0.18**	0.25**	-0.0039	-0.11	0.074	-0.040	0.23***	0.11		0.0050	-0.091
		(0.011)	(0.058)	(0.094)	(0.064)	(0.069)	(0.092)	(0.047)	(0.066)	(0.078)		(0.059)	(0.078)
	Trade, repair, transportation, … (ISIC 7-9)	0.020	0.13**	0.057	-0.00062	-0.11	0.099	0.011	0.19***	0.18*		-0.028	-0.041
		(0.011)	(0.045)	(0.074)	(0.063)	(0.057)	(0.065)	(0.047)	(0.055)	(0.080)		(0.061)	(0.065)
	All other service activities (ISIC 10-21)	0.064***	0.21***	0.11	0.027	-0.057	-0.000069	0.0055	0.14	0.16*		-0.043	-0.046
		(0.011)	(0.055)	(0.10)	(0.062)	(0.095)	(0.062)	(0.052)	(0.075)	(0.082)		(0.064)	(0.068)
	N	37888	1386	853	3917	1081	2105	2522	521	1104	691	1581	1171

Table 2.A2.2. **Impact of employment status, occupation and industry on job satisfaction, overall and by country** (cont.)

	ASIA						
	Bangladesh	Cambodia	Jordan	Lebanon	Nepal	Viet Nam**	West Bank and Gaza Strip
Self-employed (Ref. Wage employee)	0.026	0.11***		0.064	0.16**	-0.0040	-0.064
	(0.055)	(0.031)		(0.049)	(0.053)	(0.025)	(0.052)
Medium skilled / Services (ISCO 4-5)	-0.058	0.043	0.074*	-0.057	-0.066	-0.041	-0.0076
	(0.058)	(0.046)	(0.034)	(0.040)	(0.086)	(0.029)	(0.051)
Medium skilled / Agriculture (ISCO 6)	-0.060	0.049	0.042		-0.22	-0.063	0.16
	(0.078)	(0.065)	(0.12)		(0.12)	(0.058)	(0.13)
Medium skilled / Manufacturing (ISCO 7-8)	0.00035	-0.028	0.038	-0.056	-0.10	-0.048	-0.019
	(0.057)	(0.049)	(0.039)	(0.052)	(0.094)	(0.033)	(0.058)
Low skilled (ISCO 9)	-0.15*	-0.030	0.0062	-0.12	-0.12	-0.11**	-0.041
	(0.064)	(0.055)	(0.045)	(0.093)	(0.10)	(0.040)	(0.060)
Manufacturing, mining, etc. (ISIC 2-6)	-0.047	0.14***	0.044	-0.12	0.069	-0.011	0.069
	(0.050)	(0.043)	(0.093)	(0.11)	(0.080)	(0.034)	(0.080)
Trade, repair, transportation, … (ISIC 7-9)	-0.016	0.12*	0.046	-0.18	-0.039	-0.024	0.017
	(0.052)	(0.049)	(0.094)	(0.10)	(0.087)	(0.035)	(0.085)
All other service activities (ISIC 10-21)	-0.0073	0.17**	0.077	-0.10	0.0023	-0.030	0.059
	(0.058)	(0.053)	(0.093)	(0.10)	(0.092)	(0.039)	(0.086)
N	1933	2608	2440	639	552	2110	1462

Occupation: Ref. High skilled (ISCO 1-3)
Industry: ref. Agriculture and fishery (ISIC 1)

	LATIN AMERICA AND CARIBBEAN					
	Brazil	Colombia*	Dominican Republic	El Salvador*	Jamaica	Peru
Self-employed (Ref. Wage employee)	0.099**	0.037	-0.095*	0.026	0.015	
	(0.035)	(0.033)	(0.048)	(0.045)	(0.051)	
Medium skilled / Services (ISCO 4-5)	-0.12***	-0.0033	-0.051	0.039	-0.092	0.056
	(0.035)	(0.032)	(0.065)	(0.072)	(0.051)	(0.063)
Medium skilled / Agriculture (ISCO 6)	-0.18	0.17	-0.11	0.037	0.071	0.25
	(0.16)	(0.13)	(0.10)	(0.094)	(0.11)	(0.25)
Medium skilled / Manufacturing (ISCO 7-8)	-0.12**	0.056	-0.15*	0.031	-0.028	0.034
	(0.043)	(0.047)	(0.074)	(0.080)	(0.068)	(0.078)
Low skilled (ISCO 9)	-0.14***	-0.015	-0.053	0.016	-0.034	-0.074
	(0.041)	(0.045)	(0.073)	(0.076)	(0.066)	(0.074)
Manufacturing, mining, etc. (ISIC 2-6)	0.081	0.025	0.057	-0.034	-0.085	-0.061
	(0.059)	(0.14)	(0.068)	(0.062)	(0.11)	(0.13)
Trade, repair, transportation, … (ISIC 7-9)	0.050	-0.015	0.089	-0.029	0.015	-0.10
	(0.055)	(0.14)	(0.066)	(0.051)	(0.10)	(0.13)
All other service activities (ISIC 10-21)	0.039	0.016	-0.012	-0.016	0.013	-0.090
	(0.056)	(0.14)	(0.070)	(0.054)	(0.11)	(0.13)
N	1626	3128	973	1956	908	670

Occupation: Ref. High skilled (ISCO 1-3)
Industry: ref. Agriculture and fishery (ISIC 1)

Table 2.A2.2. Impact of employment status, occupation and industry on job satisfaction, overall and by country *(cont.)*

				TRANSITION				
	Armenia	Kyrgyzstan	Former Yugoslav Republic of Macedonia	Moldova	Montenegro**	Russia	Serbia	Ukraine
Occupation: Ref. High skilled (ISCO 1-3) Self-employed (Ref. Wage employee)	0.084		0.10		1.46**	0.036	0.064	0.045
	(0.067)		(0.066)		(0.46)	(0.067)	(0.10)	(0.040)
Medium skilled / Services (ISCO 4-5)	-0.032	-0.064	-0.15**	-0.090	-0.65*	-0.12*	-0.086	-0.11***
	(0.048)	(0.058)	(0.051)	(0.056)	(0.30)	(0.053)	(0.059)	(0.032)
Medium skilled / Agriculture (ISCO 6)	0.11	-0.32*	-0.15	0.068	-1.81	-0.16	-0.34*	0.11
	(0.13)	(0.14)	(0.22)	(0.18)	(0.94)	(0.15)	(0.14)	(0.077)
Medium skilled / Manufacturing (ISCO 7-8)	-0.072	-0.13*	-0.30***	-0.037	-0.39	-0.18**	-0.13	-0.059
	(0.062)	(0.064)	(0.067)	(0.068)	(0.40)	(0.061)	(0.068)	(0.035)
Low skilled (ISCO 9)	0.017	-0.23*	-0.0047	0.038	-1.18	-0.20**	-0.037	-0.25***
	(0.064)	(0.11)	(0.079)	(0.080)	(0.66)	(0.079)	(0.076)	(0.054)
Industry: ref. Agriculture and fishery (ISIC 1) Manufacturing, mining, etc. (ISIC 2-6)	0.39***	-0.032	0.49***	0.057	0.092	0.12	-0.049	0.19*
	(0.10)	(0.13)	(0.11)	(0.086)	(0.36)	(0.095)	(0.12)	(0.078)
Trade, repair, transportation, … (ISIC 7-9)	0.31**	-0.079	0.39***	0.10	-0.071	0.13	-0.10	0.15*
	(0.10)	(0.13)	(0.11)	(0.083)	(0.26)	(0.091)	(0.12)	(0.078)
All other service activities (ISIC 10-21)	0.42***	-0.022	0.48***	0.094		0.10	-0.020	0.19*
	(0.100)	(0.13)	(0.12)	(0.086)		(0.092)	(0.12)	(0.078)
N	1048	1039	675	404	258	860	566	1688

Note: The table displays average marginal effects estimated from a Probit model with the adjusted measure of satisfaction (i.e. a dummy equal to 1 if a young worker is satisfied with his/her job and does not want to change jobs) as the dependent variable. Column headers indicate the subpopulation on which the analysis focuses, and explanatory variables are listed in rows. This table presents only the results from a subset of all explanatory variables used in the regression analysis. The results relating to the other explanatory variables are provided in Table 2.A2.1 and Table 2.A2.3. Due to the inclusion of standardised monthly income as an explanatory variable, the analysis de facto excludes unpaid family workers. By and large, the conclusions hold when monthly income is dropped from the analysis and unpaid family workers are accounted for. In addition to the variables displayed in the tables, survey year and country fixed effects are also included as explanatory variables in the specifications where all countries are pulled together (corresponding to the column header "Overall"). Estimations for Montenegro, Togo and Viet Nam do not account for sampling weights as they are missing in the data. The analysis for Colombia and El Salvador refer to the urban population only. For the statistical analysis at the country level, all available rounds of the SWTS are used, and survey year fixed effects are included as additional control variables when this applies. Statistically significant coefficients at the 99.9%, 99% and 95% confidence levels are respectively indicated by ***, ** and *. The number of observations is indicated by N.

Source: Own calculations based on School-to-Work Transition Surveys 2012-2015, ILO.

Table 2.A2.3. Impact of various facets of employment on job satisfaction, overall and by country

		OVERALL (All 32 countries)	AFRICA										
			Benin	Congo	Egypt	Liberia	Madagascar	Malawi	Tanzania	Togo**	Tunisia	Uganda	Zambia
	Monthly income (standardised)	0.0100***	-0.019	-0.013		0.014	0.032	0.013	-0.063*	0.014	0.00095	0.0012	-0.0073
		(0.0024)	(0.013)	(0.012)		(0.0095)	(0.018)	(0.0091)	(0.026)	(0.021)	(0.019)	(0.0087)	(0.0073)
	Number of hours worked per week	0.00060***	0.0014*	0.0013*	0.00063	-0.00030	0.00023	0.00069	0.00014	0.0015*	0.0034**	0.0024***	-0.00031
		(0.00011)	(0.00072)	(0.00064)	(0.00040)	(0.00070)	(0.00040)	(0.00056)	(0.00078)	(0.00062)	(0.0010)	(0.00051)	(0.00028)
	Unregistered activity (Ref. Registered)	-0.056***	-0.11	-0.0019	-0.022	-0.052	-0.0074	0.00058	-0.051	-0.20**	-0.062	-0.10	-0.24***
		(0.0073)	(0.062)	(0.055)	(0.019)	(0.054)	(0.055)	(0.039)	(0.054)	(0.069)	(0.044)	(0.053)	(0.052)
	No training at work	-0.023**	-0.11	-0.15	-0.055	0.038	0.15*	-0.028	0.024	-0.18**	-0.063	0.14**	-0.052
		(0.0075)	(0.076)	(0.11)	(0.032)	(0.062)	(0.065)	(0.048)	(0.066)	(0.065)	(0.063)	(0.051)	(0.054)
	Not working while studying	0.046***		0.053	0.018	0.083*	0.064	-0.013	-0.017	0.0076	0.040	0.0012	0.012
		(0.0058)		(0.034)	(0.017)	(0.039)	(0.034)	(0.025)	(0.055)	(0.046)	(0.037)	(0.025)	(0.036)
Relevance of education: Ref. "Yes, my studies are relevant to the job"	No, overqualified	-0.20***	-0.10*	-0.14**	-0.43***	-0.22***	-0.13**	-0.15***	-0.031		-0.31***	-0.15***	-0.084
		(0.0071)	(0.049)	(0.045)	(0.019)	(0.054)	(0.045)	(0.027)	(0.066)		(0.040)	(0.039)	(0.049)
	No, underqualified	-0.082***	-0.12***	-0.15***	-0.22***	-0.19***	-0.0073	-0.059*	0.011		-0.020	-0.047	0.024
		(0.0070)	(0.032)	(0.043)	(0.064)	(0.034)	(0.036)	(0.024)	(0.048)		(0.057)	(0.031)	(0.039)
Time to find current job: Ref. Less than a week	Between a week and a month	-0.017*	0.027	0.012	0.024	-0.075	0.011	-0.024	0.081	-0.058	-0.075	-0.00068	0.10
		(0.0070)	(0.062)	(0.057)	(0.019)	(0.055)	(0.046)	(0.047)	(0.074)	(0.041)	(0.059)	(0.035)	(0.055)
	Between a month and 3 months	-0.0087	0.069*	-0.017	0.040*	-0.10*	0.038	-0.034	0.16*	-0.047	-0.00021	-0.013	0.15**
		(0.0066)	(0.034)	(0.050)	(0.019)	(0.049)	(0.048)	(0.041)	(0.068)	(0.042)	(0.051)	(0.034)	(0.046)
	More than 6 months	-0.040***	0.044	-0.060	-0.048*	-0.080	-0.061	-0.042	0.048	-0.059	-0.050	-0.0069	0.017
		(0.0068)	(0.034)	(0.052)	(0.022)	(0.048)	(0.044)	(0.038)	(0.060)	(0.036)	(0.045)	(0.030)	(0.039)
Likelihood to keep current job: Ref. very likely	Likely, but not certain	-0.25***	-0.25***	-0.21***	-0.21***	-0.18***	-0.28***	-0.18***	-0.32***	-0.31***	-0.22***	-0.22***	-0.21***
		(0.0058)	(0.033)	(0.040)	(0.017)	(0.039)	(0.044)	(0.028)	(0.045)	(0.031)	(0.033)	(0.030)	(0.043)
	Not likely	-0.37***	-0.40***	-0.32***	-0.20***	-0.10	-0.49***	-0.15***	-0.25***	-0.42***	-0.33***	-0.24***	-0.21***
		(0.0085)	(0.047)	(0.046)	(0.026)	(0.053)	(0.031)	(0.024)	(0.058)	(0.064)	(0.051)	(0.033)	(0.044)
	N	37888	1386	853	3917	1081	2105	2522	521	1104	691	1581	1171

Table 2.A2.3. **Impact of various facets of employment on job satisfaction, overall and by country** (cont.)

		ASIA						
		Bangladesh	Cambodia	Jordan	Lebanon	Nepal	Viet Nam**	West Bank and Gaza Strip
	Monthly income (standardised)	0.088**	0.011	0.0093	-0.0072	-0.012	0.016	0.100**
		(0.028)	(0.010)	(0.0080)	(0.012)	(0.018)	(0.012)	(0.034)
	Number of hours worked per week	0.0019**	0.0015**	0.00056	0.0015	0.0012	0.00062	0.00022
		(0.00061)	(0.00052)	(0.00061)	(0.00093)	(0.0012)	(0.00039)	(0.00065)
	Unregistered activity (Ref. Registered)	-0.14***	-0.056*	-0.037	-0.018	-0.21***	-0.061*	-0.037
		(0.034)	(0.028)	(0.029)	(0.052)	(0.060)	(0.025)	(0.035)
Relevance of education: Ref. "Yes, my studies are relevant to the job"	No training at work		0.038	0.019	0.023	-0.018	0.0093	-0.039
			(0.082)	(0.029)	(0.039)	(0.089)	(0.029)	(0.036)
	Not working while studying	0.13	0.0098	-0.023	-0.027		0.095***	0.057*
		(0.11)	(0.022)	(0.035)	(0.036)		(0.023)	(0.029)
	No, overqualified	-0.16**	-0.066**	-0.26***	-0.25***	-0.013	-0.19***	-0.20***
		(0.050)	(0.025)	(0.034)	(0.046)	(0.060)	(0.034)	(0.031)
	No, underqualified	-0.11**	-0.032	-0.033	0.0057	-0.0036	-0.095**	0.017
		(0.035)	(0.023)	(0.042)	(0.083)	(0.052)	(0.029)	(0.067)
Time to find current job: Ref. Less than a week	Between a week and a month	0.025	-0.028	0.020	0.080	0.063	-0.015	0.0041
		(0.035)	(0.023)	(0.027)	(0.054)	(0.069)	(0.027)	(0.044)
	Between a month and 3 months	-0.068*	-0.022	-0.0057	0.011	-0.0016	-0.028	0.020
		(0.031)	(0.030)	(0.030)	(0.051)	(0.059)	(0.027)	(0.037)
	More than 6 months	-0.081*	-0.057	-0.037	0.034	-0.029	-0.047	0.00045
		(0.032)	(0.039)	(0.032)	(0.053)	(0.060)	(0.033)	(0.037)
Likelihood to keep current job: Ref. very likely	Likely, but not certain	-0.29***	-0.36***	-0.26***	-0.35***	-0.27***	-0.39***	-0.28***
		(0.026)	(0.024)	(0.023)	(0.051)	(0.053)	(0.029)	(0.033)
	Not likely	-0.46***	-0.57***	-0.46***	-0.22	-0.57***	-0.73***	-0.43***
		(0.064)	(0.035)	(0.033)	(0.17)	(0.032)	(0.046)	(0.043)
	N	1933	2608	2440	639	552	2110	1462

Table 2.A2.3. Impact of various facets of employment on job satisfaction, overall and by country (cont.)

		LATIN AMERICA AND CARIBBEAN					
		Brazil	Colombia*	Dominican Republic	El Salvador*	Jamaica	Peru
	Monthly income (standardised)		0.10***	0.099***	0.026	-0.0019	0.0093
			(0.023)	(0.025)	(0.015)	(0.014)	(0.018)
	Number of hours worked per week	0.000085		0.00087	0.00013	0.00063	-0.0015
		(0.00069)		(0.00063)	(0.00086)	(0.00070)	(0.0011)
	Unregistered activity (Ref. Registered)	-0.18***	-0.068	-0.023	-0.078	0.057	
		(0.037)	(0.038)	(0.042)	(0.040)	(0.047)	
	No training at work	0.011		-0.25	0.015	-0.050	-0.027
		(0.030)		(0.13)	(0.061)	(0.064)	(0.046)
	Not working while studying	-0.029		-0.00075	0.072*	0.038	
		(0.080)		(0.036)	(0.033)	(0.039)	
Relevance of education: Ref. "Yes, my studies are relevant to the job"	No, overqualified	-0.20***	-0.27***	-0.070	-0.12**	-0.20***	-0.20***
		(0.032)	(0.047)	(0.100)	(0.045)	(0.043)	(0.058)
	No, underqualified	-0.094*	-0.12**	-0.13*	-0.22***	-0.053	-0.14*
		(0.038)	(0.037)	(0.055)	(0.064)	(0.056)	(0.062)
Time to find current job: Ref. Less than a week	Between a week and a month	-0.016	-0.051	0.081	-0.075	-0.055	0.069
		(0.035)	(0.034)	(0.042)	(0.040)	(0.059)	(0.052)
	Between a month and 3 months	-0.017	-0.11**	-0.021	-0.012	-0.14**	-0.013
		(0.029)	(0.038)	(0.044)	(0.041)	(0.051)	(0.047)
	More than 6 months	-0.040	-0.029	-0.078	-0.041	-0.16***	0.039
		(0.030)	(0.057)	(0.049)	(0.045)	(0.047)	(0.076)
Likelihood to keep current job: Ref. very likely	Likely, but not certain	-0.29***	-0.13***	-0.36***	-0.20***	-0.12**	-0.18***
		(0.031)	(0.026)	(0.040)	(0.034)	(0.043)	(0.048)
	Not likely	-0.44***	-0.36***	-0.47***	-0.34***	-0.43***	-0.31***
		(0.037)	(0.045)	(0.064)	(0.074)	(0.033)	(0.063)
	N	1626	3128	973	1956	908	670

Table 2.A2.3. **Impact of various facets of employment on job satisfaction, overall and by country** (cont.)

	TRANSITION							
	Armenia	Kyrgyzstan	Former Yugoslav Republic of Macedonia	Moldova	Montenegro**	Russia	Serbia	Ukraine
Monthly income (standardised)	-0.0048	0.0069	-0.00058	0.073***	-0.033	-0.0046	-0.0055	0.056**
	(0.016)	(0.018)	(0.020)	(0.021)	(0.097)	(0.014)	(0.016)	(0.021)
Number of hours worked per week	0.00055	-0.0011	0.000098		0.0030	-0.00032	0.0012	0.00022
	(0.00099)	(0.0010)	(0.0017)		(0.0081)	(0.0048)	(0.0012)	(0.00064)
Unregistered activity (Ref. Registered)	-0.17*	0	-0.33**	-0.037	-2.04**		-0.27***	-0.100
	(0.071)	(.)	(0.11)	(0.13)	(0.62)		(0.078)	(0.077)
No training at work	0.014	0.032	-0.026	0.012	-0.070	-0.024	0.023	0.027
	(0.069)	(0.065)	(0.059)	(0.058)	(0.22)	(0.044)	(0.046)	(0.030)
Not working while studying	0.11*	0.082	0.051	-0.013	0.12	0.039	0.044	0.064**
	(0.044)	(0.042)	(0.044)	(0.041)	(0.23)	(0.041)	(0.053)	(0.025)
No, overqualified	-0.24***	-0.20***	-0.33***	-0.069	-0.80**	-0.20***	-0.31***	-0.17***
	(0.047)	(0.048)	(0.050)	(0.054)	(0.25)	(0.050)	(0.043)	(0.050)
No, underqualified	0.076	-0.11*	0.044	-0.0060	0	-0.093	-0.11	-0.11**
	(0.068)	(0.053)	(0.083)	(0.053)	(.)	(0.052)	(0.092)	(0.040)
Between a week and a month	0.0020	-0.19***	-0.10	0.019	0.25	0.084	-0.14*	-0.031
	(0.052)	(0.048)	(0.073)	(0.060)	(0.50)	(0.053)	(0.065)	(0.036)
Between a month and 3 months	-0.026	-0.039	-0.052	-0.016	-0.13	0.12*	-0.0038	-0.019
	(0.044)	(0.043)	(0.066)	(0.057)	(0.32)	(0.050)	(0.064)	(0.033)
More than 6 months	-0.089	-0.16**	-0.0033	0.059	-0.30	-0.042	-0.050	-0.10*
	(0.046)	(0.060)	(0.055)	(0.082)	(0.28)	(0.059)	(0.055)	(0.043)
Likely, but not certain	-0.11*	-0.033	-0.21***	0.071	0.062	-0.11**	-0.21***	-0.18***
	(0.053)	(0.046)	(0.044)	(0.047)	(0.25)	(0.040)	(0.045)	(0.033)
Not likely	-0.18**	-0.13*	-0.39***	-0.22***	-1.47***	-0.28***	-0.44***	-0.63***
	(0.067)	(0.053)	(0.062)	(0.064)	(0.34)	(0.072)	(0.064)	(0.043)
N	1048	1039	675	404	258	860	566	1688

Row-group labels (reading down the left margin): **Relevance of education: Ref. "Yes, my studies are relevant to the job"** (No, overqualified / No, underqualified); **Time to find current job: Ref. Less than a week** (Between a week and a month / Between a month and 3 months / More than 6 months); **Likelihood to keep current job: Ref. very likely** (Likely, but not certain / Not likely).

Note: The table displays average marginal effects estimated from a Probit model with the adjusted measure of satisfaction (i.e. a dummy equal to 1 if a young worker is satisfied with his/her job and does not want to change jobs) as the dependent variable. Column headers indicate the subpopulation on which the analysis focuses, and explanatory variables are listed in rows. This table presents only the results from a subset of all explanatory variables used in the regression analysis. The results relating to the other explanatory variables are provided in Table 2.A2.1 and Table 2.A2.2. Due to the inclusion of standardised monthly income as an explanatory variable, the analysis de facto excludes unpaid family workers. By and large, the conclusions hold when monthly income is dropped from the analysis and unpaid family workers are accounted for. In addition to the variables displayed in the tables, survey year and country fixed effects are also included as explanatory variables in the specifications where all countries are pulled together (corresponding to the column header "Overall"). Estimations for Montenegro, Togo and Viet Nam do not account for sampling weights as they are missing in the data. The analysis for Colombia and El Salvador refer to the urban population only. For the statistical analysis at the country level, all available rounds of the SWTS are used, and survey year fixed effects are included as additional control variables when this applies. Statistically significant coefficients at the 99.9%, 99% and 95% confidence levels are respectively indicated by ***, ** and *. The number of observations is indicated by N.

Source: Own calculations based on School-to-Work Transition Surveys 2012-2015, ILO.

Table 2.A2.4. Results by area of residence and gender

		All sample	Urban	Rural	Male	Female
Occupation: Ref. High skilled (ISCO 1-3)	Self-employed (Ref. Wage employee)	0.066***	0.072***	0.066***	0.050***	0.093***
		(0.0071)	(0.011)	(0.011)	(0.0096)	(0.012)
	Medium skilled / Services (ISCO 4-5)	-0.026**	-0.029**	-0.018	-0.032**	-0.025*
		(0.0082)	(0.010)	(0.015)	(0.011)	(0.012)
	Medium skilled / Agriculture (ISCO 6)	-0.036**	-0.078***	-0.021	-0.069***	0.00074
		(0.013)	(0.023)	(0.019)	(0.017)	(0.021)
	Medium skilled / Manufacture (ISCO 7-8)	-0.026**	-0.025*	-0.031	-0.042***	-0.0053
		(0.0094)	(0.012)	(0.016)	(0.012)	(0.016)
	Low skilled (ISCO 9)	-0.081***	-0.080***	-0.079***	-0.11***	-0.045**
		(0.010)	(0.013)	(0.017)	(0.013)	(0.016)
Industry: Ref. Agriculture (ISIC 1)	Manufacturing, mining,.. (ISIC 2-6)	0.043***	0.043*	0.041**	0.050***	0.030
		(0.011)	(0.018)	(0.015)	(0.014)	(0.019)
	Trade, Repair, Transportation… (ISIC 7-9)	0.020	0.0050	0.036*	0.017	0.027
		(0.011)	(0.018)	(0.015)	(0.013)	(0.018)
	All other service activities (ISIC 10-21)	0.064***	0.060***	0.062***	0.067***	0.055**
		(0.011)	(0.018)	(0.016)	(0.014)	(0.019)
	Standardised monthly income	0.0100***	0.012***	0.0056	0.0096**	0.010*
		(0.0024)	(0.0034)	(0.0035)	(0.0030)	(0.0039)
	Number of hours worked a week	0.00060***	0.00056***	0.00080***	0.00042**	0.00082***
		(0.00011)	(0.00016)	(0.00017)	(0.00015)	(0.00019)
	Unregistered activity (Ref. registered)	-0.056***	-0.047***	-0.065***	-0.047***	-0.067***
		(0.0073)	(0.0098)	(0.011)	(0.0090)	(0.012)
	No training at work	-0.023**	-0.031***	-0.0081	-0.029**	-0.013
		(0.0075)	(0.0094)	(0.013)	(0.0098)	(0.012)
	Not working while studying	0.046***	0.061***	0.024**	0.045***	0.047***
		(0.0058)	(0.0082)	(0.0083)	(0.0074)	(0.0090)
Ref. Yes, my education is relevant to my current job	No, I feel overqualified	-0.20***	-0.19***	-0.19***	-0.19***	-0.20***
		(0.0071)	(0.0096)	(0.010)	(0.0089)	(0.011)
	No, I feel underqualified	-0.082***	-0.081***	-0.076***	-0.073***	-0.088***
		(0.0070)	(0.010)	(0.0092)	(0.0089)	(0.010)

Table 2.A2.4. **Results by area of residence and gender** *(cont.)*

		All sample	Urban	Rural	Male	Female
Time to find current job: **Ref. Less than a week**	Between a week and a month	-0.017*	-0.014	-0.021*	-0.016	-0.021
		(0.0070)	(0.0095)	(0.010)	(0.0090)	(0.011)
	Between a month and 3 months	-0.0087	-0.0062	-0.011	-0.011	-0.0059
		(0.0066)	(0.0089)	(0.0100)	(0.0084)	(0.010)
	More than 6 months	-0.040***	-0.044***	-0.034***	-0.038***	-0.040***
		(0.0068)	(0.0093)	(0.0100)	(0.0088)	(0.010)
Ref.- very likely to keep this job	Likely, but not certain	-0.25***	-0.23***	-0.24***	-0.24***	-0.23***
		(0.0058)	(0.0068)	(0.0081)	(0.0066)	(0.0081)
	Not likely	-0.37***	-0.36***	-0.33***	-0.36***	-0.33***
		(0.0085)	(0.012)	(0.012)	(0.011)	(0.013)
	Age (in years)	0.00014	0.0021*	-0.0018	0.0016	-0.0016
		(0.00064)	(0.00092)	(0.00092)	(0.00084)	(0.0010)
	Female (Ref. Male)	0.00041	0.0012	-0.0027		
		(0.0048)	(0.0067)	(0.0072)		
	Rural (Ref. Urban)	0.0048			0.012	-0.0055
		(0.0054)			(0.0070)	(0.0085)
Household financial situation: **Ref. Well-off**	Fairly well-off	-0.021	-0.033*	-0.0079	-0.026	-0.018
		(0.012)	(0.015)	(0.020)	(0.015)	(0.020)
	Average	-0.088***	-0.10***	-0.063***	-0.086***	-0.091***
		(0.011)	(0.014)	(0.019)	(0.014)	(0.019)
	Fairly poor	-0.15***	-0.17***	-0.12***	-0.15***	-0.15***
		(0.012)	(0.016)	(0.020)	(0.015)	(0.020)
	Very poor	-0.20***	-0.20***	-0.18***	-0.19***	-0.20***
		(0.013)	(0.018)	(0.021)	(0.017)	(0.021)

Table 2.A2.4. **Results by area of residence and gender** (cont.)

		All sample	Urban	Rural	Male	Female
Father's completed education: Ref. No schooling	Primary	-0.011	0.0030	-0.023*	-0.0036	-0.024*
		(0.0069)	(0.010)	(0.0098)	(0.0089)	(0.011)
	Secondary general	-0.023**	-0.012	-0.033*	-0.022*	-0.024
		(0.0084)	(0.012)	(0.013)	(0.011)	(0.013)
	Vocational studies	-0.038***	-0.022	-0.052**	-0.037**	-0.039*
		(0.010)	(0.014)	(0.016)	(0.013)	(0.015)
	Tertiary	-0.011	-0.0091	0.010	-0.025	0.0068
		(0.011)	(0.014)	(0.019)	(0.014)	(0.016)
Young worker's completed education: Ref. No schooling	Primary	-0.031***	-0.044**	-0.028*	-0.029*	-0.041**
		(0.0090)	(0.015)	(0.012)	(0.012)	(0.015)
	Secondary vocational	-0.054***	-0.070***	-0.047**	-0.055***	-0.053*
		(0.013)	(0.020)	(0.018)	(0.016)	(0.022)
	Secondary general	-0.061***	-0.077***	-0.056***	-0.065***	-0.058***
		(0.0098)	(0.016)	(0.014)	(0.013)	(0.017)
	Post-secondary vocational	-0.082***	-0.098***	-0.075**	-0.10***	-0.057**
		(0.013)	(0.019)	(0.023)	(0.017)	(0.022)
	Graduate	-0.087***	-0.096***	-0.11***	-0.10***	-0.066**
		(0.012)	(0.018)	(0.020)	(0.016)	(0.021)
	Post-graduate	-0.11***	-0.11***	-0.14***	-0.16***	-0.066*
		(0.022)	(0.029)	(0.040)	(0.031)	(0.034)
Ref. No health issues	At least one health issue	-0.049***	-0.059***	-0.041***	-0.054***	-0.041***
		(0.0079)	(0.011)	(0.011)	(0.011)	(0.011)
	N	37888	19948	16944	22182	15706

Note: The table displays average marginal effects estimated from a Probit model with adjusted measure of satisfaction as the dependent variable and pooling all countries together. Column headers indicate the subpopulation on which the analysis focuses, namely all young workers and then urban, rural, female and male young workers. Due to the inclusion of standardised monthly income as an explanatory variable, the analysis de facto excludes unpaid family workers. The conclusions do not change when monthly income is dropped from the analysis. Based on the International Standard Industry Classification (ISIC), industries are aggregated in four categories: agriculture, forestry and fishing (ISIC 1), manufacturing, mining, electricity and water supply related activities and construction (ISIC 2-6), wholesale and retail trade, repair, transportation and storage, accommodation and food services activities (ISCI 7-9), and other services activities including information, communication, finance, real estate, administrative services, education etc. (ISIC 10 to 21). In addition to the variables displayed in the table, explanatory variables include year and country fixed effects for all specifications. Due to the absence of weights' variable for Montenegro, Togo and Viet Nam, the weights are never used in the above specifications. Statistically significant coefficients at the 99.9%, 99% and 95% confidence levels are respectively indicated by ***, ** and *.

Source: Own calculations based on School-to-Work Transition Surveys 2012-2015, ILO.

Table 2.A2.5. **Results by employment status**

		Employee	Self-employed	Unpaid family worker
	Limited contract period (Ref. Unlimited)	-0.041***		
		(0.012)		
	Oral agreement (Ref. Written)	-0.11***		
		(0.013)		
	Unregistered activity (Ref. Registered)	-0.031*	-0.099**	
		(0.015)	(0.036)	
Ref. Very likely to keep current job	Likely, but not certain	-0.25***	-0.27***	-0.29***
		(0.012)	(0.020)	(0.020)
	Not likely	-0.39***	-0.28***	-0.33***
		(0.019)	(0.022)	(0.026)
Ref. Yes, my education is relevant to my current job	No, I feel overqualified	-0.23***	-0.12***	-0.16***
		(0.015)	(0.025)	(0.025)
	No, I feel underqualified	-0.11***	-0.059**	-0.050**
		(0.019)	(0.019)	(0.017)
	Standardised monthly income	0.0088	0.0095	
		(0.0057)	(0.0074)	
	Number of hours worked a week	0.00050	0.0011**	0.00091*
		(0.00026)	(0.00034)	(0.00041)
Reasons for the employment status: Ref. "Could not find a wage job"	More independence		0.15***	
			(0.020)	
	More flexible working hours		0.13***	
			(0.033)	
	Higher income		0.16***	
			(0.025)	
	Required by the family		0.058*	0.21***
			(0.024)	(0.019)
	Learning the family business			0.21***
				(0.030)
Occupation: Ref. High skilled (ISCO 1-3)	Medium skilled / Services (ISCO 4-5)	-0.054***	-0.048	-0.016
		(0.016)	(0.034)	(0.071)
	Medium skilled / Agriculture (ISCO 6)	-0.039	-0.032	-0.14
		(0.032)	(0.041)	(0.075)
	Medium skilled / Manufacture (ISCO 7-8)	-0.020	-0.055	-0.080
		(0.018)	(0.037)	(0.074)
	Low skilled (ISCO 9)	-0.11***	-0.025	-0.078
		(0.022)	(0.041)	(0.073)
Industry: Ref. Agriculture (ISIC 1)	Manufacturing, mining,.. (ISIC 2-6)	0.042	0.059	0.013
		(0.023)	(0.043)	(0.050)
	Trade, Repair, Transportation… (ISIC 7-9)	0.038	0.036	-0.056
		(0.024)	(0.033)	(0.049)
	All other service activities (ISIC 10-21)	0.054*	-0.0046	0.033
		(0.025)	(0.034)	(0.042)
	Age (in years)	-0.0018	-0.0028	0.0026
		(0.0014)	(0.0021)	(0.0018)
	Female (Ref. Male)	-0.011	-0.0021	0.041**
		(0.010)	(0.015)	(0.015)
	Rural (Ref. Urban)	-0.0062	-0.0018	-0.013
		(0.011)	(0.017)	(0.020)

Table 2.A2.5. **Results by employment status** (cont.)

		Employee	Self-employed	Unpaid family worker
Household financial situation: Ref. Well-off	**Fairly well-off**	-0.038	-0.054	0.10*
		(0.021)	(0.064)	(0.045)
	Average	-0.10***	-0.095	0.044
		(0.020)	(0.055)	(0.042)
	Fairly poor	-0.17***	-0.13*	0.031
		(0.022)	(0.056)	(0.044)
	Very poor	-0.25***	-0.19***	-0.031
		(0.028)	(0.056)	(0.044)
Father's completed education: Ref. No schooling	**Primary**	-0.021	-0.020	0.0048
		(0.014)	(0.019)	(0.021)
	Secondary general	-0.032	-0.059*	0.025
		(0.020)	(0.026)	(0.032)
	Vocational studies	-0.053**	-0.015	0.011
		(0.018)	(0.037)	(0.041)
	Tertiary	-0.022	0.015	-0.027
		(0.019)	(0.034)	(0.048)
Young worker's completed education: Ref. No schooling	**Primary**	-0.066***	-0.070***	-0.059**
		(0.015)	(0.018)	(0.022)
	Secondary vocational	-0.11***	-0.039	-0.16***
		(0.022)	(0.054)	(0.035)
	Secondary general	-0.14***	-0.077**	-0.16***
		(0.019)	(0.026)	(0.030)
	Post-secondary vocational	-0.18***	-0.15***	-0.16*
		(0.024)	(0.044)	(0.068)
	Graduate	-0.18***	-0.12**	-0.24***
		(0.022)	(0.038)	(0.048)
	Post-graduate	-0.21***	-0.14	-0.11
		(0.032)	(0.088)	(0.14)
Ref. No health issues	**At least one health issue**	-0.031	-0.026	-0.0024
		(0.017)	(0.021)	(0.023)
	N	23548	11710	10083

Note: The table displays average marginal effects estimated from a Probit model with adjusted measure of satisfaction as the dependent variable and pooling all countries together. The set of explanatory variables varies with the subpopulation (indicated in the column headers) on which the analysis focuses, namely wage employees, self-employed workers and unpaid family workers. Based on the International Standard Industry Classification (ISIC), industries are aggregated in four categories: agriculture, forestry and fishing (ISIC 1), manufacturing, mining, electricity and water supply related activities and construction (ISIC 2-6), wholesale and retail trade, repair, transportation and storage, accommodation and food services activities (ISCI 7-9), and other services activities including information, communication, finance, real estate, administrative services, education, etc. (ISIC 10 to 21). In addition to the variables displayed in the table, explanatory variables include year and country fixed effects for all three specifications. Due to the absence of weights' variable for Montenegro, Togo and Viet Nam, the weights are never used in the above specifications. Statistically significant coefficients at the 99.9%, 99% and 95% confidence levels are respectively indicated by ***, ** and *.

Source: Own calculations based on School-to-Work Transition Surveys 2012-2015, ILO.

From youth employment preferences to jobs reality in developing countries

Accounts of well-being based on preference satisfaction or desire fulfilment say that people experience greater well-being to the extent that their preferences are satisfied or their desires are fulfilled. This chapter considers two aspects of subjective well-being in the sense of preference satisfaction that were discussed earlier: youth career aspirations and facets of job satisfaction. It then asks a simple question: How likely are these employment preferences to be satisfied given the reality of jobs in developing countries? The chapter starts by confronting youth employment preferences with realistic employment prospects. It then discusses the implications that a large gap in youth employment preference may have for public policy.

The question about the extent to which youth career aspirations are aligned with the reality of the labour market is critical to understanding youth well-being, firms' productivity and youth labour-market performance. For youth, this aspect of well-being depends on the degree to which one's preference is satisfied or one's desire fulfilled. Assuming that youth well-being is sufficiently correlated with or causally efficacious in bringing about greater preference satisfaction (Angner, 2012), then it is reasonable to believe that young people whose career preferences reflect realistic opportunities in the labour market would be better off, insofar as their career preferences are more likely to be satisfied. Beyond the direct cost of not fulfilling a desire, unrealistic aspirations can further entail the indirect cost of leaving youth inadequately equipped to cope with the reality of the labour market. Career preference satisfaction is also relevant for employers. Firms where employees are able to fulfil their job-related goals and aspirations tend to experience greater employee motivation, which leads to better productivity (Mann, Massey and Glover, 2013). A good alignment between youth career aspirations and the reality of jobs is also an indication that the youth labour market is working effectively in signalling to young people the type of opportunities that are available. To ensure a smooth school-to-work transition, it is necessary to help youth make well-informed decisions about how many years to study, which subject to choose or what type of initial work experience to seek. In contrast, broad misalignment in career aspirations and job opportunities may lead to low motivation, frustration or, worse, social unrest and large migration outflows.

Confronting youth career aspirations with the reality of the labour market

Youth career aspirations appear to be overly optimistic in light of today's and tomorrow's labour market needs. Evidence from the School-to-Work Transition Surveys (SWTS) shows that on average across countries, and in all 32 single countries that are covered by the surveys, a large majority of students want to work in a high-skilled occupation (80%), few want to take on a medium-skilled job (18%), and even fewer want to work in a low-skilled job (3%). However, only 20% of all young workers currently occupy a high-skilled job, while 66% hold a medium-skilled job and 15% have a low-skilled job (Figure 3.1). Accordingly, and holding all else constant, this indicates that 60% of the students wishing to work in a high-skilled occupation will most likely not fulfil their career aspirations, while as many as 73% of young workers in medium-skilled jobs and 80% in low-skilled jobs may not have been able to satisfy their career preferences. Considering that structural transformation may affect these estimates by increasing the demand for skilled labour, a similar exercise can be performed using the International Labour Organization (ILO) overall employment projections by skills level in 2021. The foresight analysis yields similar results and points to a large misalignment in youth career preferences and projected labour demand (Annex 3.A1, Figure 3.A1.1).

Career aspiration gaps are wide everywhere, but the depth differs across world regions, with challenge of unrealistic career aspirations most challenging in Africa and Latin America. On average, the gap between the share of students wanting to work in high-skilled occupations and the actual share of highly skilled young workers amounts to 54% in transition economies and 58% in Asian countries (Figure 3.1). The gap is still broader in Africa (65%) and in Latin American and the Caribbean (62%). Within world regions in general, the richer the country, the smaller the gap, as the share of high-skilled occupations tends to increase with the level of economic development. This is the case for Tunisia in Africa for example, but also for Lebanon and Jordan in Asia, and for Armenia and Ukraine in transition economies. A few poor countries, such as Benin, Malawi and Cambodia, also have relatively small career aspiration gaps, due to a relatively low share of students aspiring to work in high-skilled occupations.

Figure 3.1. Difference between the distribution of aspirations and the distribution of workers at different skills levels of the occupations by country (%)

Panel A. High skilled occupations (ISCO 1-3)

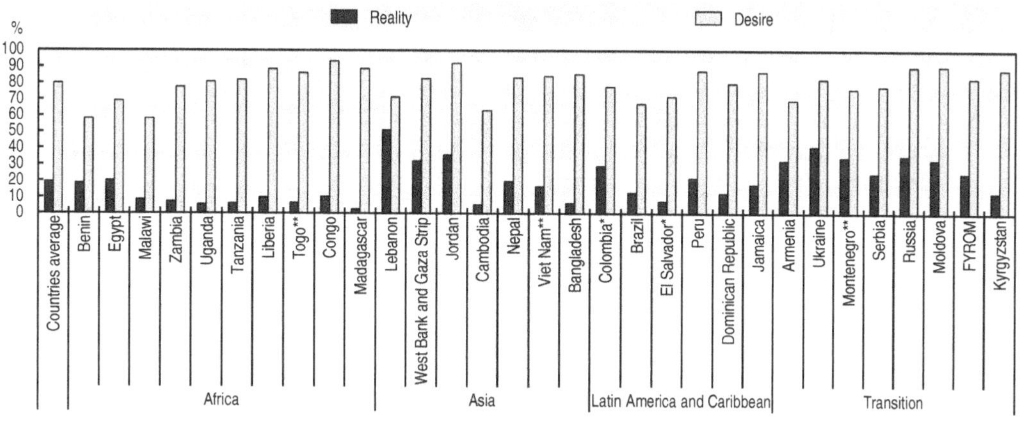

Panel B. Medium skilled occupations (ISCO 4-8)

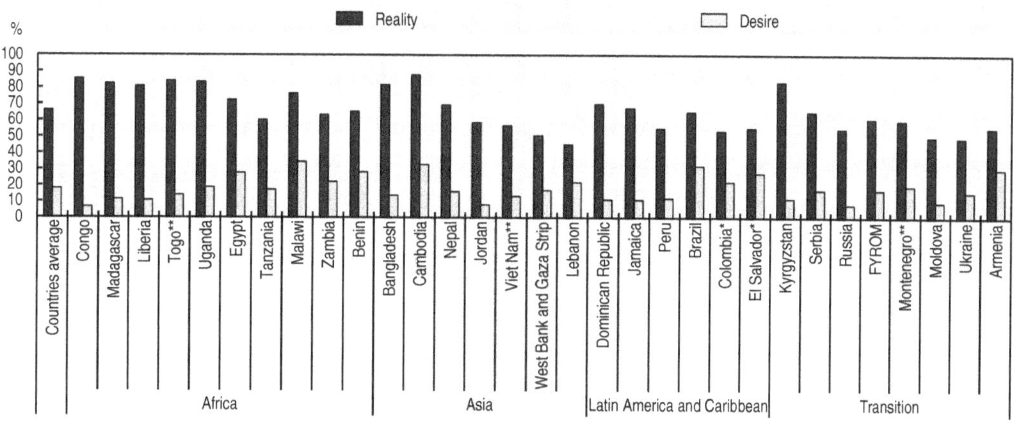

Panel C. Low skilled occupations (ISCO 9)

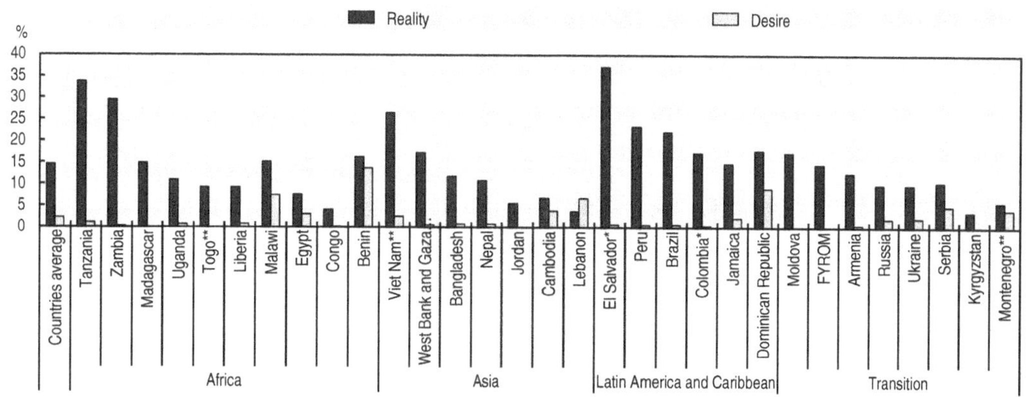

Note: Countries are sorted by the difference between the share of young students who say they want to work in a high skilled (Panel A), medium skilled (Panel B) or low skilled (Panel C) occupation and the proportion of these categories in the 15-29 working population. Data are missing for Tunisia. FYROM corresponds to Former Yugoslav Republic of Macedonia.

* Data for Colombia and El Salvador refer to the urban population only.

** Estimations for Montenegro, Togo and Viet Nam do not account for sampling weights as they are missing in the data.

Source: Own calculations based on School-to-Work Transition Surveys 2012-2015, ILO.

A major concern is that the gap between youth career aspirations and the reality of the labour market persists for tertiary-educated students. Figure 3.2 reproduces the information presented above but focuses on students enrolled in tertiary education and young workers who have completed tertiary education. As such, it restricts the analysis to a population that a priori possesses the level of qualification required for a high-skilled occupation. The results show that the share of students declaring that they would like to work in high-skilled occupations is still much higher than the actual share of tertiary-educated young workers engaged in these occupations. The difference reaches 48% on average across countries, meaning that around 48% of tertiary-educated students wishing to work legitimately in a high-skilled job are unlikely to be able to do so. This indicates that reconciling the career aspirations of an ever increasing population of graduates with the capacity to produce high-skilled jobs is a major challenge in many developing and emerging countries. It also suggests that providing well-informed and early guidance on the opportunities and potential difficulties prevailing in the labour market can contribute to bringing young people closer to their aspirations.

While career aspirations of tertiary-educated students are similar across countries, the mismatch with the reality of jobs is less pronounced in more developed economies where employment opportunities for the highly skilled are greater. In most countries, the size of the high- skilled sector drives the degree of matching between aspirations and reality. While on average in each world region, around 90% of tertiary students want to work in a high-skilled occupation, there are large differences in the share of the tertiary population actually working in a high-skilled occupation (Figure 3.2). In Africa, only 36% of youth who completed tertiary education are engaged in a high- skilled occupation, compared to 59% in LAC and around 65% in transition and Asian economies. Within each region, richer and more developed economies have larger highly skilled sectors, and therefore smaller gaps between career aspirations and the reality of the labour market.

Africa stands out as the region with the largest share of tertiary-educated workers engaged in medium- or low-skilled jobs. On average across countries, a large share of tertiary-educated youth works in medium-skilled (40%) or even low-skilled (5%) occupations (Figure 3.2). The phenomenon is particularly important in Africa, where the share of highly educated youth working in medium-skilled occupations ranges from to 86% in Liberia and 73% in Malawi to 38% in Egypt and 44% in Tanzania. While no students enrolled in tertiary education wish to work in a low-skilled occupation (with the noticeable exception of Cambodia), many of them will nonetheless end up in such occupations. In Africa, this is the case for up to 27% of young workers in Zambia, 13% in Togo and 10% in Malawi. In other world regions, a high share of tertiary-educated workers in low-skilled jobs is also observed in Peru (9%), El Salvador (8.5%) and West Bank and Gaza Strip (7.5%). These findings suggest that unlocking the potential of youth entrepreneurship among tertiary-educated youth, in particular in Africa, could create an interesting opportunity for students to use their skills efficiently, provided that well-designed entrepreneurship programmes are made easily accessible.

Figure 3.2. Youth career aspiration gaps for high-skilled occupations among tertiary-educated youth (%)

Panel A. High skilled occupations (ISCO 1-3)

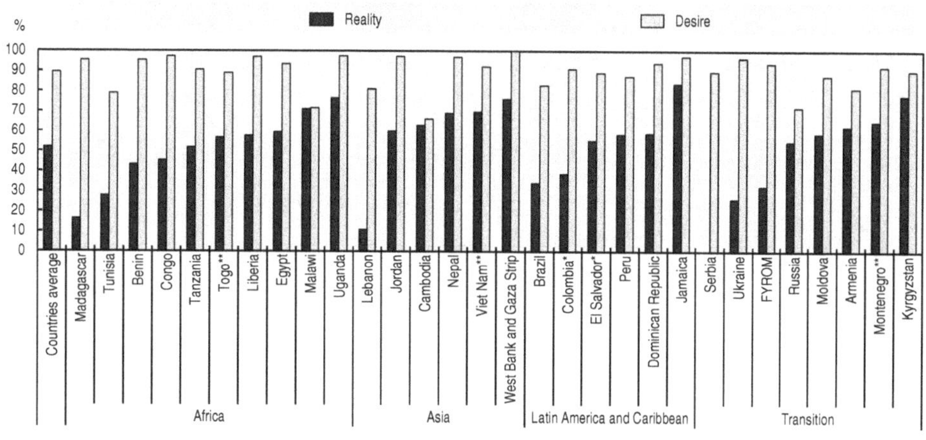

Panel B. Medium skilled occupations (ISCO 4-8)

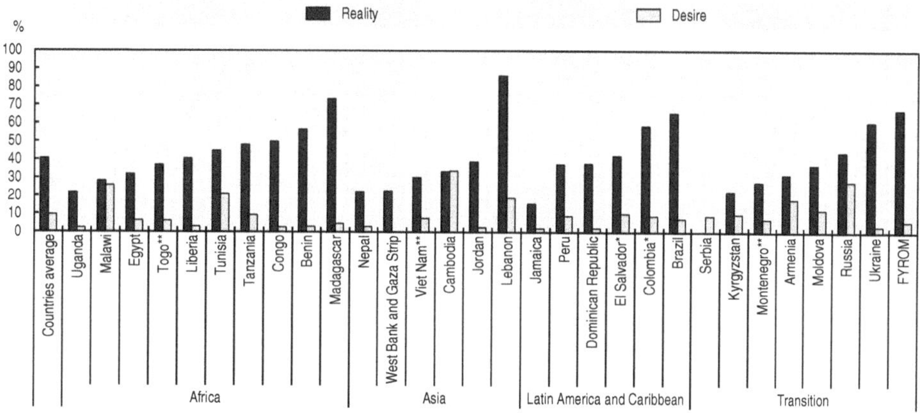

Panel C. Low skilled occupations (ISCO 9)

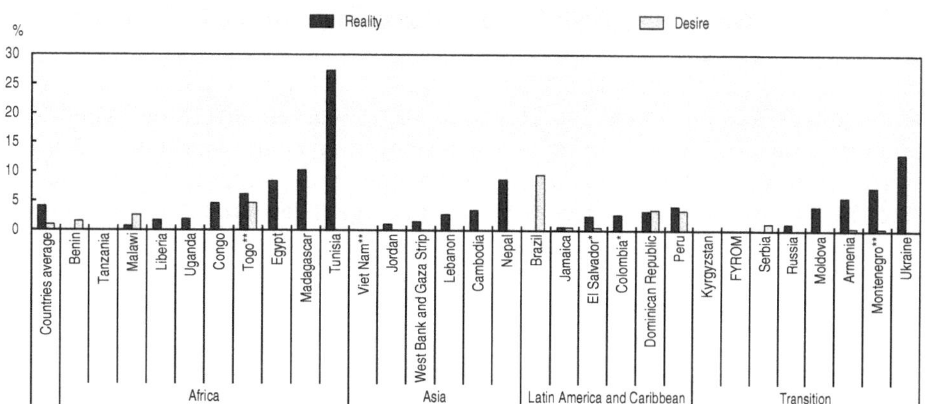

Note: Countries are sorted by the difference between the share of young students who say they want to work in a high skilled (Panel A), medium skilled (Panel B) or low skilled (Panel C) occupation and the proportion of these categories in the 15-29 working population for tertiary-educated individuals. Data are missing for Tunisia. As the proportion of tertiary students is small in many developing countries, these estimates have been calculated using small samples and therefore should be viewed with caution. FYROM corresponds to Former Yugoslav Republic of Macedonia.

* Data for Colombia and El Salvador refer to the urban population only.

** Estimations for Montenegro, Togo and Viet Nam do not account for sampling weights as they are missing in the data.

Source: Own calculations based on School-to-Work Transition Surveys 2012-2015, ILO.

Remarkably, students' career aspirations do not always reflect earning differentials across occupations. On average across countries, high-skilled occupations pay 0.1 standard deviation (SD) more than medium-skilled occupations and 0.2 standard deviation more than low-skilled occupations (Figure 3.3). Yet there are large differences across countries in the returns to occupations on the labour market. In 9 out of 32 countries (Armenia, Benin, Kyrgyzstan, Lebanon, Liberia, Peru, Tanzania, Ukraine and West Bank and Gaza Strip), average earnings are higher for medium-skilled and/or low-skilled occupations than for high-skilled occupations. This suggests that earnings differentials do not always explain the large misalignment in career aspirations and the reality of jobs.

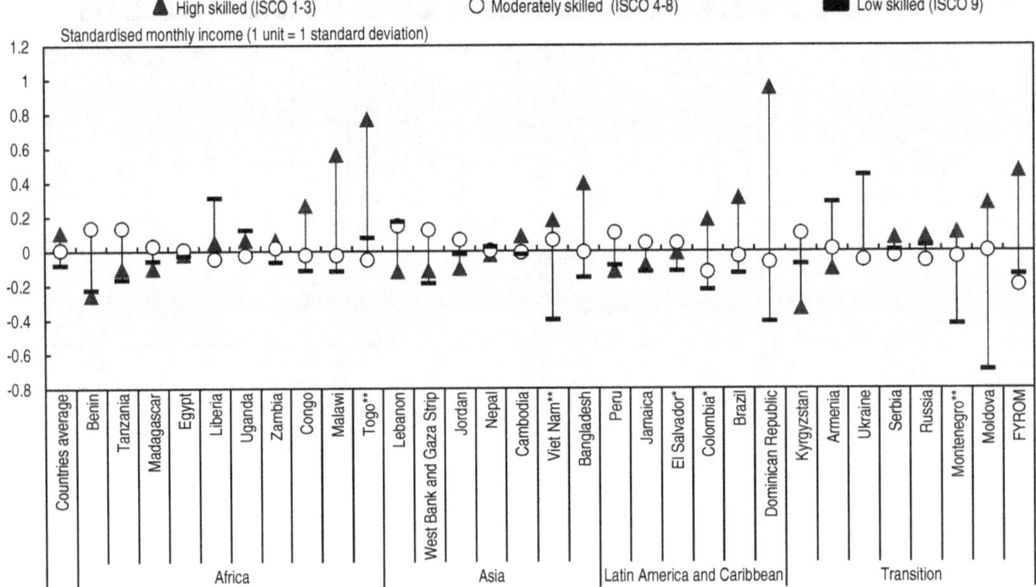

Figure 3.3. **High skilled occupations do not always pay higher wages**

Note: Countries are sorted by the average monthly income observed for young workers engaged in high-skilled occupations within each group. Data are missing for Tunisia. FYROM corresponds to Former Yugoslav Republic of Macedonia.

* Data for Colombia and El Salvador refer to the urban population only.

** Estimations for Montenegro, Togo and Viet Nam do not account for sampling weights as they are missing in the data.

Source: Own calculations based on School-to-Work Transition Surveys 2012-2015, ILO.

The attractiveness of the public sector exceeds by far the employment opportunities it provides. While around 57% of students express the desire to work for the public sector on average across countries, the public sector accounts for a maximum of just 17% of employment among young workers (including workers at state-owned enterprises), potentially leaving 40% of young people with unmet aspirations (Figure 3.4). In contrast, the private sector accounts for 60% of youth employment while only 20% of young students said they wanted to work in this sector on average. These unbalances are likely to affect education choices and translate into phenomena such as job queuing in the public sector, which is largely observed in developing and emerging countries (see for instance Hyder, 2007, for Pakistan, and Mengistae, 1999, for Ethiopia). In this respect, extending youth access to social protection in the non-state sector and encouraging formal labour relations could reinforce the attractiveness of the private sector.

Self-employment appears to be more attractive to students in transition and LAC countries than the employment opportunities it represents, while in Africa the opposite is true. In Africa, with the exception of Egypt, the prevalence of youth entrepreneurship exceeds by far the share of young people wishing to become self-employed. This contrasts with LAC and transition countries, where becoming self-employed is a job-related goal reported by a much larger share of young people than the actual proportion of young workers in self-employment. In Asia, there is no such regional trend. The difference between the share of young workers in self-employment and the share of students wishing to become self-employed is positive in countries like Viet Nam and Cambodia, negative in Lebanon and Bangladesh, and close to zero in Jordan, the Palestinian Authority, and Nepal.

Figure 3.4. **Aspirations in terms of sector of activity**

Panel A. Self-employment (family business)

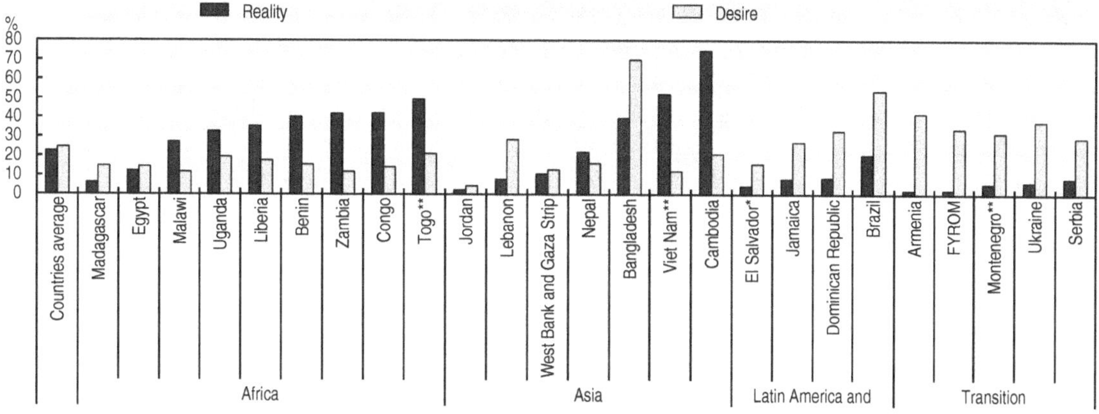

Panel B. Public sector (international organisations, NGOs)

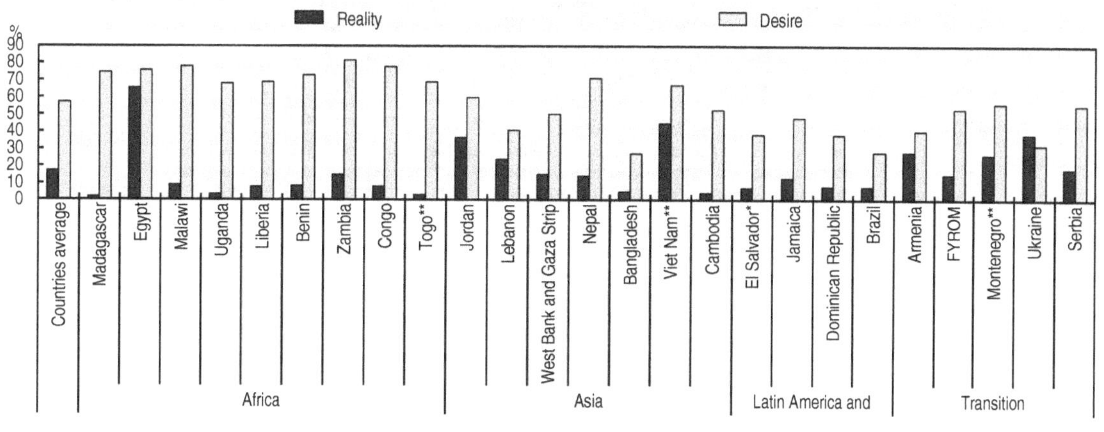

Panel C. Private sector

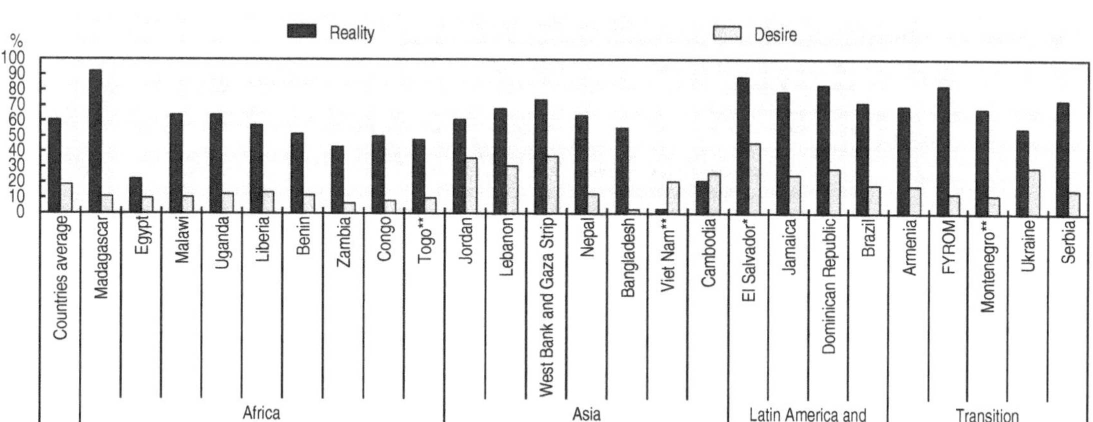

Note: Countries are sorted by the difference between the share of young students who say they want to work in self-employment (Panel A) within each country group. A similar ordering is kept for Panel B and C. In Panel B, wage employment in the public sector includes employment in international organisation, NGOs and public companies. Data are missing for Colombia, Peru, Russian Federation, Tanzania and Tunisia. FYROM corresponds to Former Yugoslav Republic of Macedonia.

* Data for El Salvador refer to the urban population only.

** Estimations for Montenegro, Togo and Viet Nam do not account for sampling weights as they are missing in the data.

Source: Own calculations based on School-to-Work Transition Surveys 2012-2015, ILO.

The challenge of matching facets of job satisfaction with the reality of job conditions

Understanding the extent to which facets of job satisfaction match the reality of job conditions has important implications for workers, employers and policy makers. A number of important job-related drivers of job satisfaction among youth were identified in the previous chapter: being self-employed and contributing to family work by choice or for family reasons; working in high-skilled occupations and outside agriculture; earnings; job security; working in the formal economy; and having the right qualification in the job. The discussion below addresses the question of whether young people in developing countries are likely to encounter many or some of these facets of job satisfaction in their working life. The question is relevant for young workers, employers and policy makers alike, as the effects of low job satisfaction can be far reaching. Empirical evidence shows that when employees are not happy with their jobs, they are much more likely to experience stress at work. Job dissatisfaction can also spread through the workplace and undermine the morale of other employees and the overall productivity of the workforce. Low job satisfaction also causes higher turnover rates with employees who, sooner or later, will quit to find a job that they actually enjoy.

Figure 3.5. **Distribution of young workers by employment status**

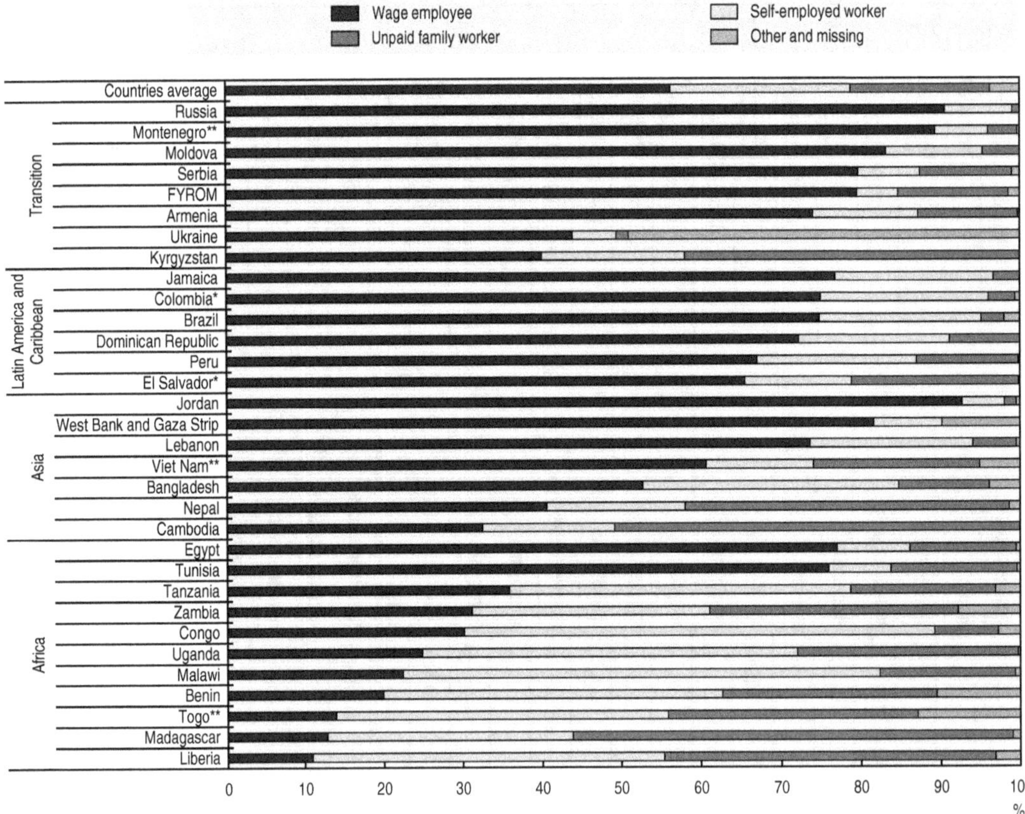

Note: Countries are sorted by the proportion of wage employees within each group. Data are missing for Tunisia.
* Data for Colombia and El Salvador refer to the urban population only. FYROM corresponds to Former Yugoslav Republic of Macedonia.
** Estimations for Montenegro, Togo and Viet Nam do not account for sampling weights as they are missing in the data.
Source: Own calculations based on School-to-Work Transition Surveys 2012-2015, ILO.

Self-employment by choice or for family reasons, a facet of job satisfaction, is a relatively common form of employment among young people aged 15-29 years in low-income countries. On average in the SWTS data, most young workers are engaged in wage employment (56%). Yet self-employment (22.5%) is much more common in the countries surveyed than in OECD member countries (Figure 3.6).[1] There are also disparities across regions. Self-employment is particularly important in sub-Saharan Africa, where it is by far the most common employment status (from 30% in Zambia to 60% in Malawi), followed by South and Southeast Asia (from 9% in Cambodia to 32% in Bangladesh) and Latin America and the Caribbean (from 13% in El Salvador to 20% in Brazil). Additional light is cast by looking at the extent to which self-employment is chosen voluntarily, for family reasons or by default. On average across countries, only 32% of young self-employed workers joined self-employment by default, i.e. because they could not find wage employment (Figure 3.7). This indicates that the remaining 68% were able to engage in a form of self-employment that constitutes an important facet of job satisfaction (by choice or required by the family). The share of young workers benefiting from these satisfying forms self-employment also varies greatly between and within world regions: in Asia, from 75% of total youth self-employed workers (Bangladesh) to 91% (Viet Nam); in LAC, from 57% (Dominican Republic) to 83 % (Peru); in Africa, from 46% (Liberia) to 83 % (Benin); and in transition countries, from 44% (Serbia) to 72% (Ukraine).

Figure 3.6. **Distribution of self-employed youth workers according to their reason for being self-employed**

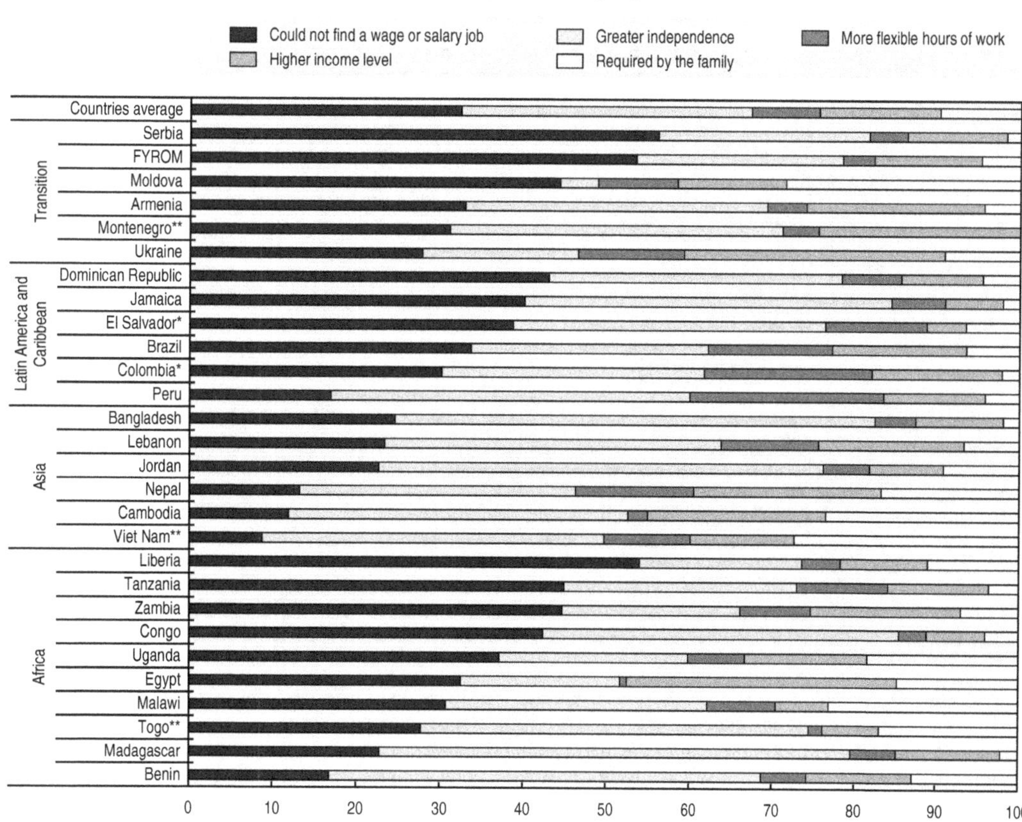

Note: Countries are sorted by the proportion of self-employed workers who could not find wage employment within each group. Data are missing for Kyrgyzstan, West Bank and Gaza Strip, Russian Federation and Tunisia.

* Data for Colombia and El Salvador refer to the urban population only. FYROM corresponds to Former Yugoslav Republic of Macedonia.

** Estimations for Montenegro, Togo and Viet Nam do not account for sampling weights as they are missing in the data.

Source: Own calculations based on School-to-Work Transition Surveys 2012-2015, ILO.

Engaging in unpaid family work, which impacts job satisfaction differently depending on the reasons for it, is not an unusual form of employment in developing countries. Contributing family workers, often referred to as unpaid family workers, engage in a specific and common form of employment in many developing countries. They are not inactive – they are actually working in the family business or activity – but do not receive an explicit payment (either in kind or cash) for their work. Usually they receive food and lodging in exchange for their contribution. Data from the SWTS show that, on average across countries, about 17.5% of all young workers were contributing family workers (Figure 3.7). Yet this average hides important disparities across and within world regions. The share of young workers in unpaid family work ranges from 8% (Republic of the Congo) to 55% (Madagascar) in Africa; from almost 0% (West Bank and Gaza Strip) to 51% (Cambodia) in Asia; from 3% (Brazil) to 21% (El Salvador) in LAC; and from less than 1% (Russian Federation) to 42% (Kyrgyzstan) in transition countries. An examination of the reasons why young people engage in unpaid family work indicates that few voluntarily choose in this status, while families play a central role. On average across countries, young people engage in family work mostly because it is required by the family (56%), and also as a way to learn the family business (17%). When unpaid family work is not a choice by default, i.e. for lack of other options, it can be associated with a higher satisfaction level than wage employment. This is the case, for example, in many African countries, where unpaid family work is widespread (see above, Figure 2.2, Panel B).

Figure 3.7. **Distribution of unpaid family workers according to their reason for joining this status**

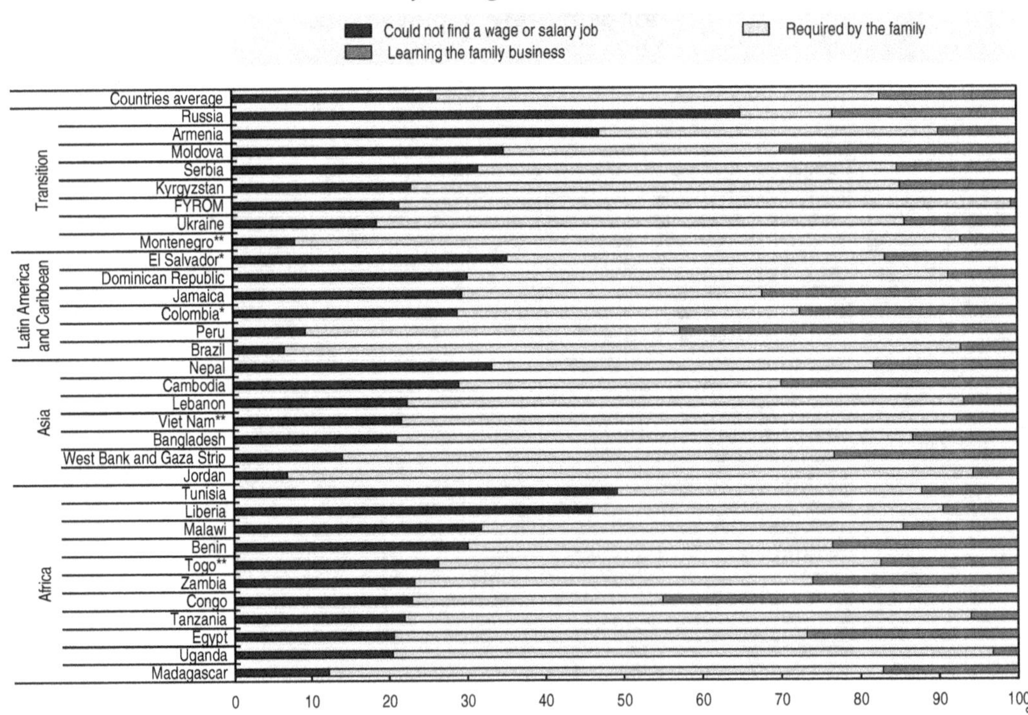

Note: Countries are sorted by the proportion of unpaid family workers who could not find wage employment within each group. FYROM corresponds to Former Yugoslav Republic of Macedonia.

* Data for Colombia and El Salvador refer to the urban population only.

** Estimations for Montenegro, Togo and Viet Nam do not account for sampling weights as they are missing in the data.

Source: Own calculations based on School-to-Work Transition Surveys 2012-2015, ILO.

While high-skilled jobs bring about greater job satisfaction, few young people in developing countries are able to take on such jobs. The distribution of workers across occupations presented in Figure 3.8 reflects both the overall structure of the economies and the types of occupations that are more accessible to young people. On average across countries, only 18% of young workers are engaged in high-skilled occupations, compared to about 67% in medium-skilled occupations and 15% in low-skilled occupations. There are large occupational differences between and within world regions, however. In transition economies and the Middle East, a relatively greater proportion of young workers are engaged in high-skilled occupations (from 13% in Kyrgyzstan to 41% in Ukraine, and from 18% in West Bank and Gaza Strip to 51% in Lebanon), and fewer youth workers are in low-skilled occupations (from 4% in Kyrgyzstan to 17% in Moldova, and from 4% in Lebanon to 23% in West Bank and Gaza Strip). This contrasts with Africa, South and South-East Asia and, remarkably, LAC, where only a small share of working young people are engaged in high-skilled occupations (from 2% in Madagascar to 20% in Benin; from 5% in Cambodia to 17% in Nepal; and from 7% in El Salvador to 29% in Colombia). Those in low skilled jobs range from 4% in Congo to 36% in Tanzania; from 7% in Cambodia to 29% in Viet Nam; and from 15% in Jamaica to 38% in El Salvador.

Figure 3.8. Distribution of young workers by qualification level of occupation

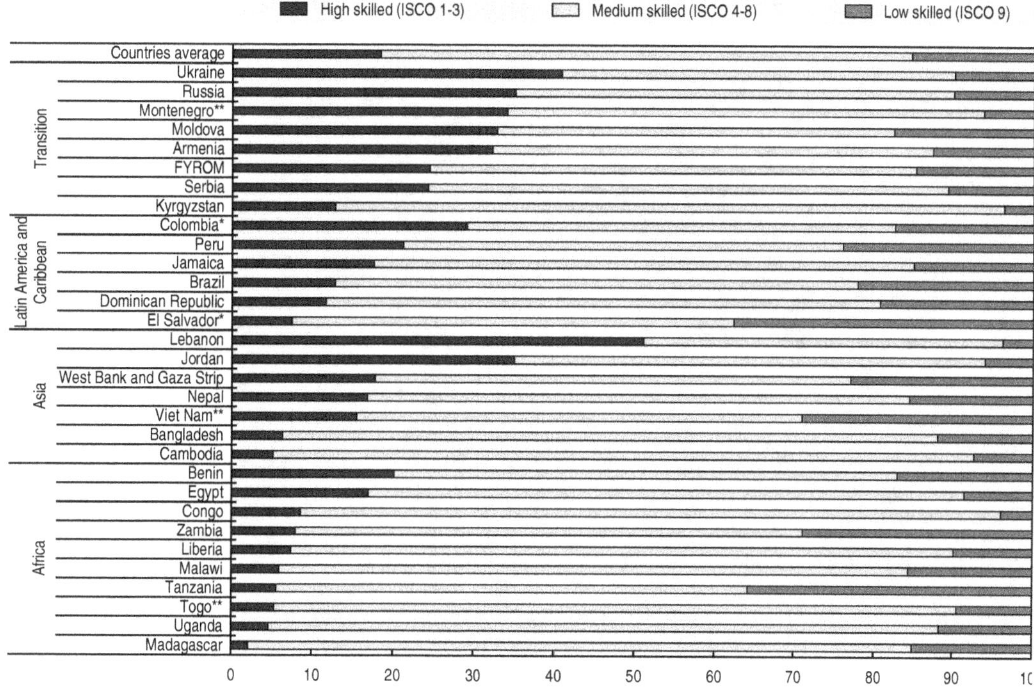

Note: Countries are sorted by the proportion of workers engaged in a high-skilled occupation within each group. Data are missing for Tunisia. FYROM corresponds to Former Yugoslav Republic of Macedonia.
* Data for Colombia and El Salvador refer to the urban population only.
** Estimations for Montenegro, Togo and Viet Nam do not account for sampling weights as they are missing in the data.
Source: Own calculations based on School-to-Work Transition Surveys 2012-2015, ILO.

Agriculture remains an important source of jobs for many young people in several countries, even though it does not produce high job satisfaction. On average across countries, the distribution of industries across young workers is quite balanced, with around 22% in agriculture, 20% in manufacturing and construction, 30% in trade and transportation, and 28% in all other services (Figure 3.9). As we have seen, young workers in agriculture are less often satisfied with their work than those in other occupations. Yet agriculture remains an important source of jobs for many young people in several countries in the developing world (AfDB/OECD/UNDP/UNECA, 2012). One out of three young workers is engaged in agriculture in a number of countries in Africa (Liberia, Madagascar, Togo and Zambia), Asia (Bangladesh and Nepal), Latin America and Caribbean (El Salvador) and in transition countries (Kyrgyzstan). This indicates the importance of investing in agriculture, improving access to markets, developing the use of information and communication technology, and supporting innovations in the sector in order to reconcile young people with agriculture and attract talented young people to agriculture-related occupations.

Figure 3.9. **Distribution of young workers by type of industry**

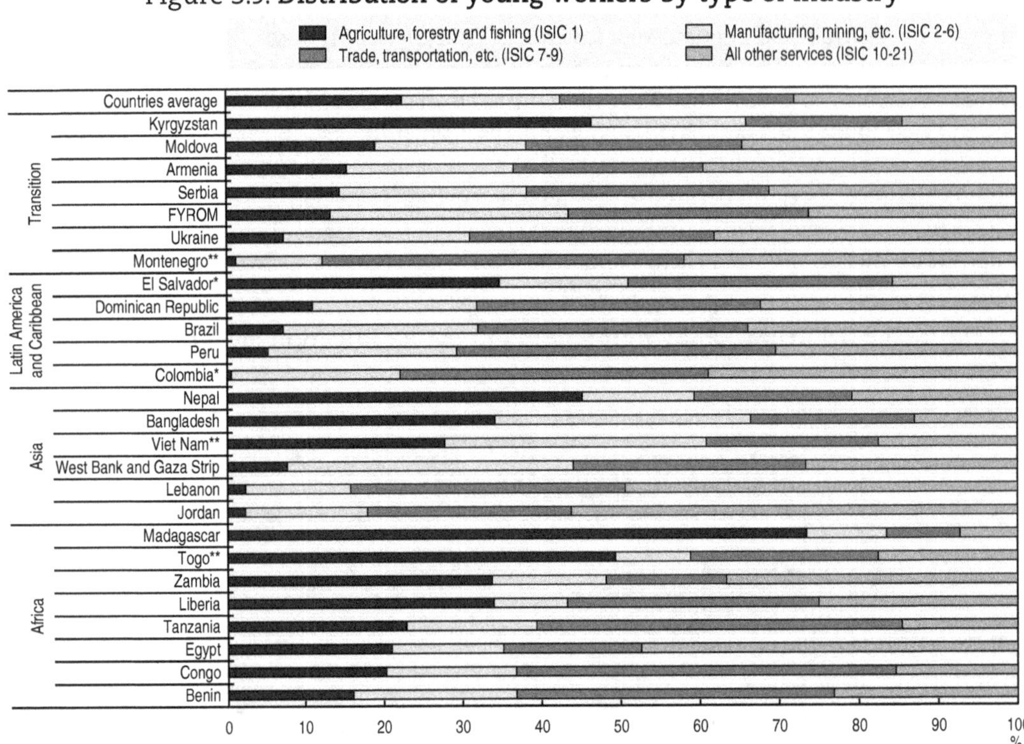

Note: Countries are sorted by the proportion of workers engaged in a high-skilled occupation within each group. Data are missing for Tunisia. Based on the International Standard Industry Classification (ISIC), industries are aggregated in four categories: agriculture, forestry and fishing (ISIC 1); manufacturing, mining, electricity and water supply related activities and construction (ISIC 2-6); wholesale and retail trade, repair, transportation and storage, accommodation and food services activities (ISCI 7-9); and other services activities including information, communication, finance, real estate, administrative services, education, etc. (ISIC 10 to 21). FYROM corresponds to Former Yugoslav Republic of Macedonia.

* Data for Colombia and El Salvador refer to the urban population only.

** Estimations for Montenegro, Togo and Viet Nam do not account for sampling weights as they are missing in the data.

Source: Own calculations based on School-to-Work Transition Surveys 2012-2015, ILO.

Low levels of job security, which drive job satisfaction down, affect a non-negligible proportion of young workers. Two indicators can be used in the SWTS to assess the level of job security among the youth workforce in developing countries. The first indicator is subjective and relates to the likelihood that the worker will keep the current employment situation over the next 12 months. The second indicator is objective, but restricted to wage employees only, and refers to the employee's type of contract (unlimited versus limited). On average across countries, and regarding the first indicator, 64% of young workers report that they are very likely to keep their current employment situation, about 25% that they are likely but not certain and 11% that it is not likely (Figure 3.10). However, the level of job security varies widely across countries. For instance, the share of young workers not likely to keep their jobs is below 5% in Bangladesh, Lebanon, Nepal and Ukraine, but above 30% in Zambia and Malawi. Regarding the second indicator, the SWTS show that, on average, 69% of young wage employees benefit from an unlimited work contract (Figure 3.11). But this average hides important disparities across regions and countries. Only 58% of youth wage employees in Africa have contracts of unlimited duration, compared to more than 70% in Asia, LAC and transition economies. Fewer than half of wage employees benefit from an unlimited contract in Egypt, Malawi, Viet Nam, Montenegro and Peru. Addressing job security concerns thus appears to be one of the most important directions toward better job satisfaction.

Figure 3.10. Likelihood of keeping the same job over the next 12 months, among all workers

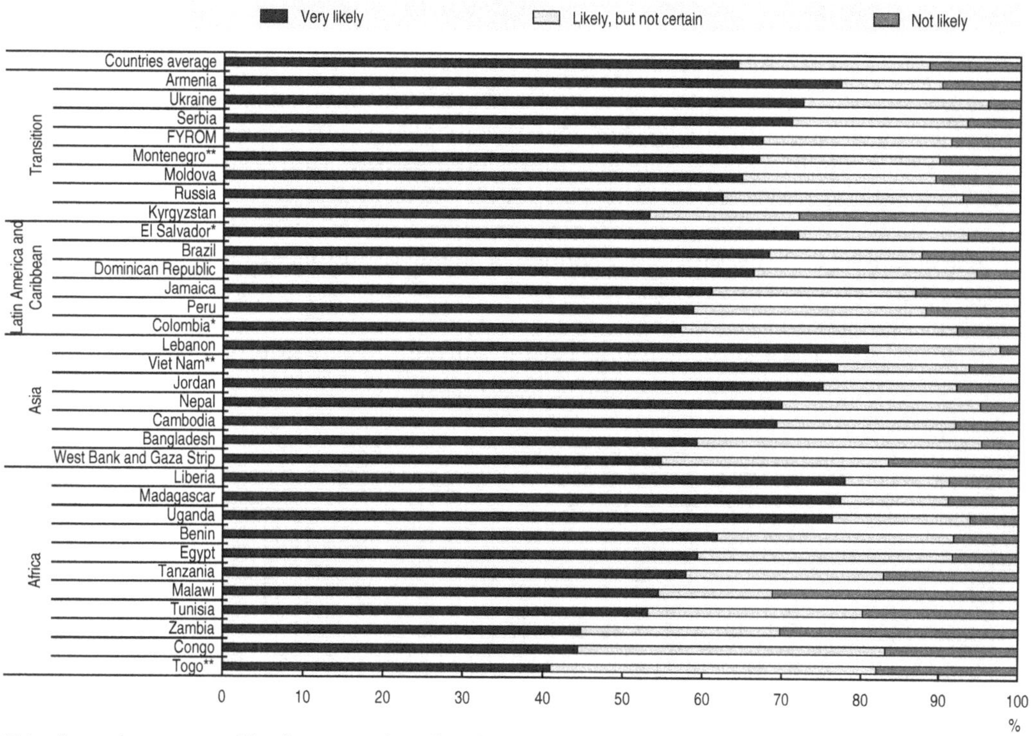

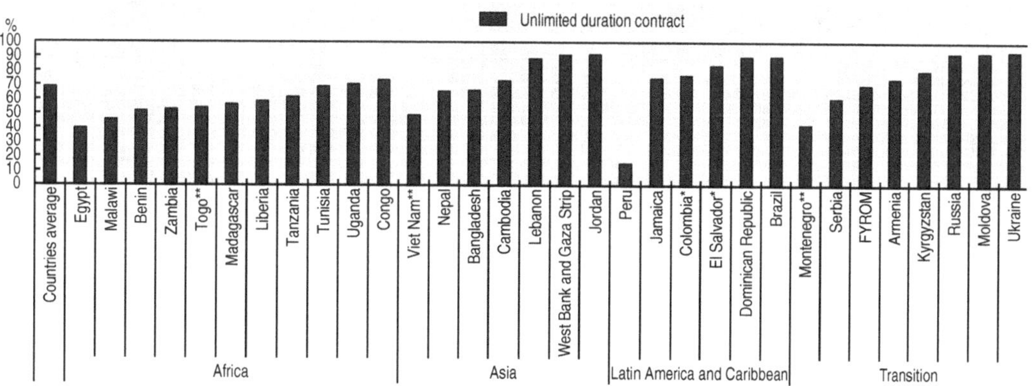

Note: Countries are sorted by the proportion of workers who think are very likely to keep their job within each group.

* Data for Colombia and El Salvador refer to the urban population only. FYROM corresponds to Former Yugoslav Republic of Macedonia.

** Estimations for Montenegro, Togo and Viet Nam do not account for sampling weights as they are missing in the data.

Source: Own calculations based on School-to-Work Transition Surveys 2012-2015, ILO.

Figure 3.11. The share of young wage employees with contracts of unlimited duration

Notes: Countries are sorted by the proportion of wage employees with an unlimited contract within each group.

* Data for Colombia and El Salvador refer to the urban population only. FYROM corresponds to Former Yugoslav Republic of Macedonia.

** Estimations for Montenegro, Togo and Viet Nam do not account for sampling weights as they are missing in the data.

Sources: Own calculations based on School-to-Work Transition Surveys 2012-2015, ILO.

While more formal labour relations raise job satisfaction, a large number of young people work in the informal economy. On average across countries, only 50% of young workers are engaged in a registered activity (Figure 3.12, Panel A). Looking beyond aggregate figures further shows large disparities across world regions. While the share of young workers engaged in a registered activity is above 80% in transition countries and about 67% in LAC, it declines to 52% in Asia and to 21% in Africa. A similar trend emerges when looking at the share of wage employees covered by a written contract. On average, only 50% of all youth wage employees are covered by a written contract, but there are large regional disparities (Figure 3.12, Panel B). In Africa and Asia, the majority of young wage employees report having only an oral agreement. In LAC countries, oral agreements are also common. Only in transition economies do few young wage employees report oral agreements.

Figure 3.12. **Informality among young workers in developing countries, %**

Panel A. Registered activity

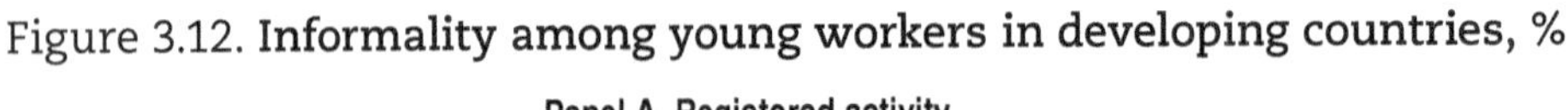
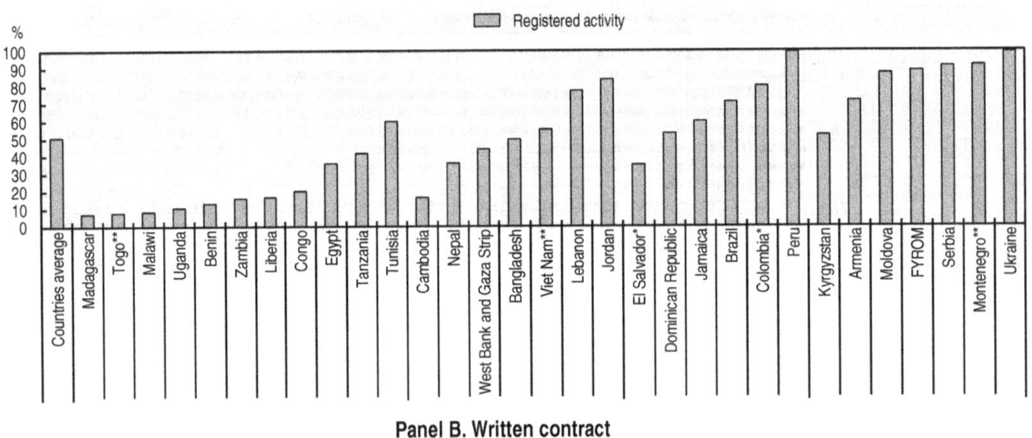

Panel B. Written contract

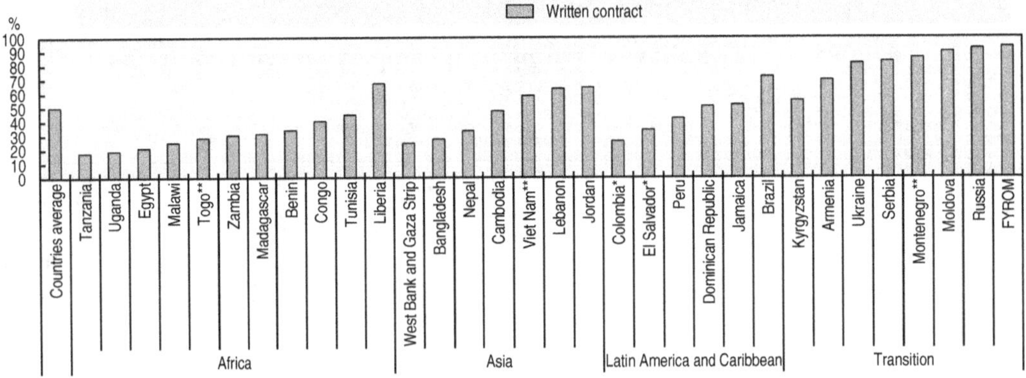

Note: Countries are sorted by the proportion of workers who work in a registered activity (Panel A) and who benefit from a written contract (Panel B) within each group. Data from the Russian Federation are missing.
* Data for Colombia and El Salvador refer to the urban population only. FYROM corresponds to Former Yugoslav Republic of Macedonia.
** Estimations for Montenegro, Togo and Viet Nam do not account for sampling weights as they are missing in the data.
Source: Own calculations based on School-to-Work Transition Surveys 2012-2015, ILO.

Many young workers experience skills mismatch, which is an important source of job dissatisfaction. Possessing qualifications and skills in line with job requirements is often seen as a crucial component of the quality of the working environment and is a strong driver of job satisfaction. There are various ways to measure the adequate level of skills and education for a given occupation. This report considers two measures. The first measure is based on a subjective assessment of the relevance of young workers' education to their current employment. The second measure refers to the normative ILO definition, which relies on a general accepted equivalence between occupations and the level of education required (ILO, 2012).[2] While the two measures need not be perfectly consistent as they highlight different aspects of the skills mismatch, comparing them shows that young workers feel more confident about the adequacy of their qualifications than what is observed based on the ILO normative measure (Annex 3.A2, Figure 3.A2.1). Both measures point to a large skills mismatch, however. According to the subjective measure, about two-thirds of young workers on average judge that their education was relevant to their job. Across world regions, feelings about qualification mismatches are higher in African countries, where only 55% of workers declare their training relevant, against 70% in transition and Asian countries, and 80% in LAC countries (Figure 3.13). The nature of the skills mismatch (overqualification versus underqualification) also varies across countries. More than one out of four young workers feels overqualified in Egypt (33%) and Tunisia (29%) in Africa; West Bank and Gaza Strip (38%) and Lebanon (28%) in Middle East Asia; and Serbia (32%) and Moldova (30%) in transition countries. At the same time, underqualification is reported by a large number of young workers in African countries such as Benin (42%), Madagascar (37%), Tanzania and Uganda (34%), Malawi and Liberia (30%), and Togo (27%), as well as in Nepal (28%) in Asia. Using a normative approach shows similar results on the skills mismatch across countries but points to a higher proportion of the phenomenon, with only 44% of adequately qualified workers on average across countries (Figure 3.14).

Figure 3.13. **Young workers' perceptions about the relevance of their education to their current job requirements**

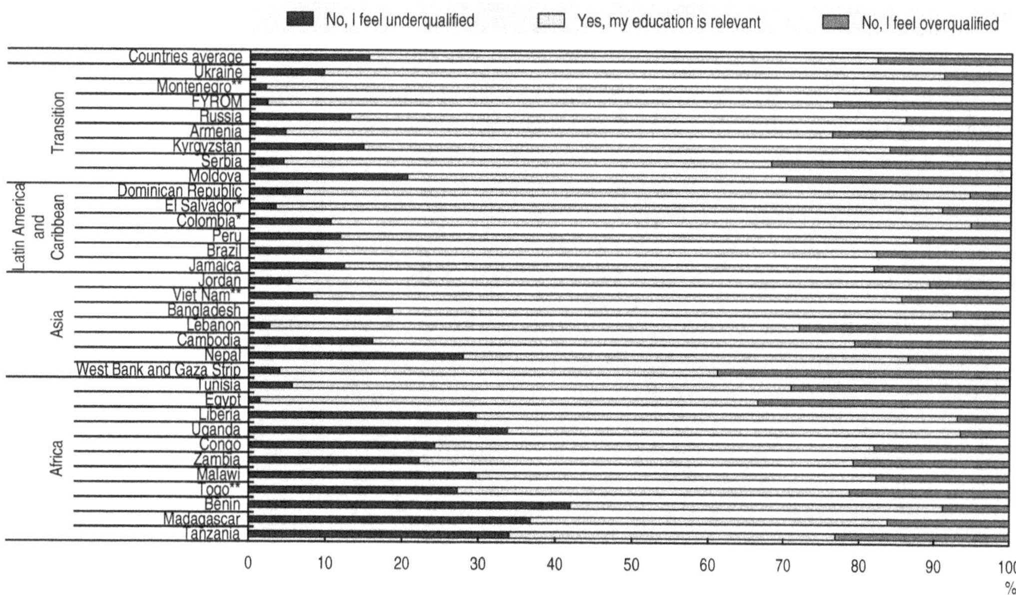

Note: Countries are sorted by the proportion of workers with feel they have relevant qualifications within each group.

* Data for Colombia and El Salvador refer to the urban population only. FYROM corresponds to Former Yugoslav Republic of Macedonia.

** Estimations for Montenegro, Togo and Viet Nam do not account for sampling weights as they are missing in the data.

Source: Own calculations based on School-to-Work Transition Surveys 2012-2015, ILO.

Figure 3.14. Qualification according to a normative mismatch measure based on the level of education required for each type of occupation, %

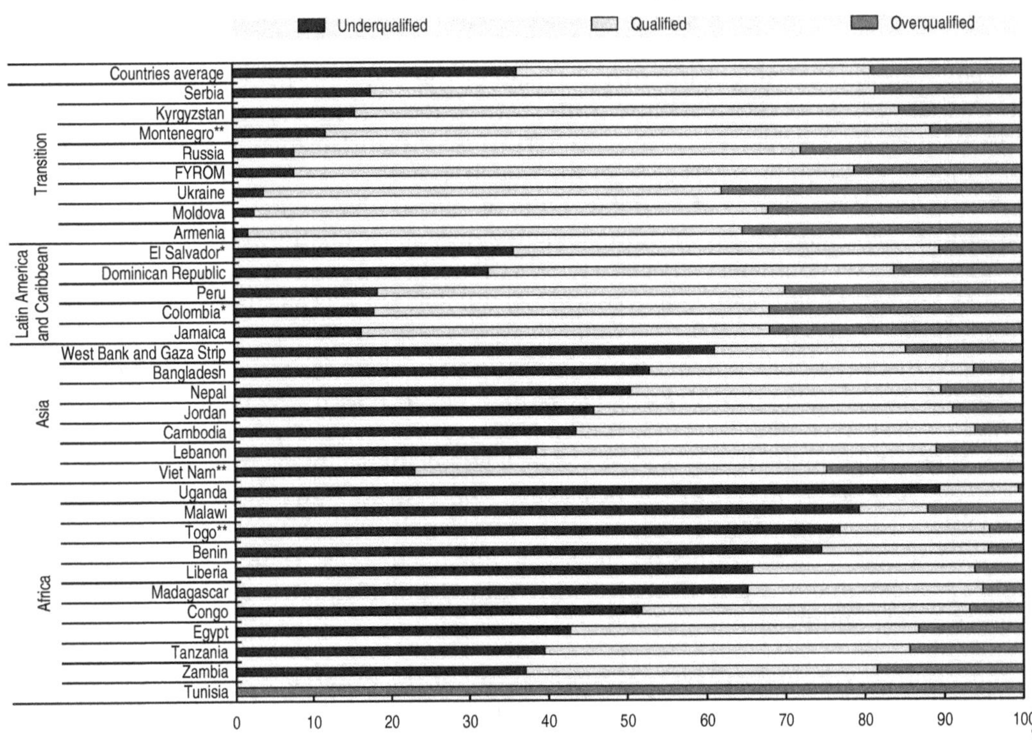

Note: Countries are sorted by the proportion of workers who are underqualified according to the normative measures within each group. The normative mismatch measure is based on a mapping of ISCO-08 major groups to ISCED skills levels as follows. An individual working in a high-skilled occupation (ISCO 1-3) should have completed at least some tertiary education, an individual working in a medium-skilled occupation (ISCO 4-8) should have completed (general or vocational) secondary education and an individual working in a low-skilled occupation (ISCO 9) should have completed at least primary education. These individuals are considered as adequately qualified and, if this is not the case, they enter into the over- or underqualified category. Data from Brazil and Tunisia are missing. FYROM corresponds to Former Yugoslav Republic of Macedonia.

* Data for Colombia and El Salvador refer to the urban population only.

** Estimations for Montenegro, Togo and Viet Nam do not account for sampling weights as they are missing in the data.

Source: Own calculations based on School-to-Work Transition Surveys 2012-2015, ILO.

As a response to the qualification mismatch, a small number of enterprises offer training opportunities, which are valued by workers. The share of young workers being offered a training opportunity is surprisingly similar across world regions. On average, around 20% of young workers benefit from such an opportunity (Figure 3.15). This is remarkably low given the importance of the skills mismatch in developing countries, even if there is wide diversity across countries. Training opportunities mainly benefit wage employees (24%), but are not inexistent among self-employed workers (14%) and unpaid family workers (11%).

Figure 3.15. **Share of young workers who are offered some training at work, by employment status (%)**

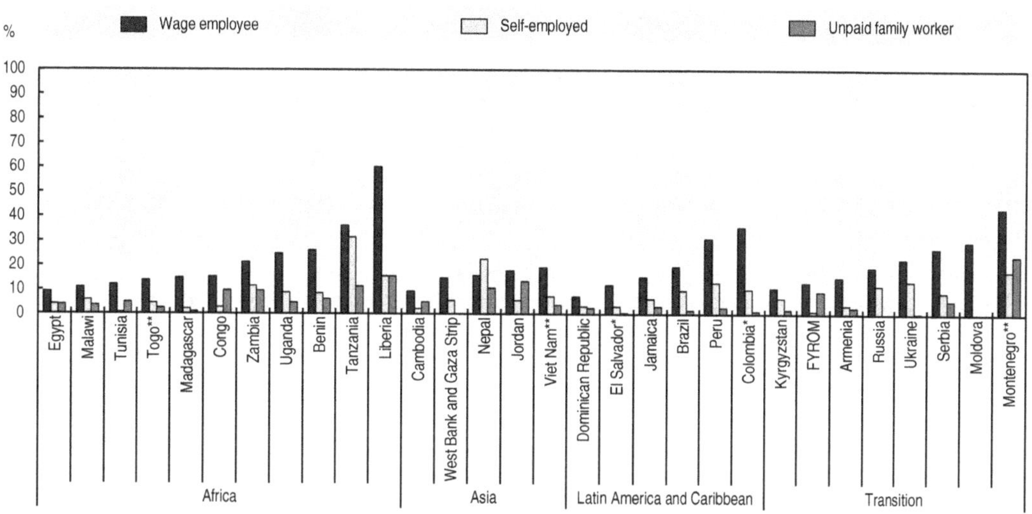

Note: Countries are sorted by the proportion of wage employees being offered some training at work within each group. Data from Bangladesh and Lebanon are missing due to inconsistency. The information on training opportunity is missing for more than 60% of observations in Dominican Republic and Jamaica. FYROM corresponds to Former Yugoslav Republic of Macedonia.

* Data for Colombia and El Salvador refer to the urban population only.

** Estimations for Montenegro, Togo and Viet Nam do not account for sampling weights as they are missing in the data.

Source: Own calculations based on School-to-Work Transition Surveys 2012-2015, ILO.

All in all, the findings of this study indicate that there is an urgent need to act now on the large gap between youth aspirations and the reality of the labour markets. Evidence from the 32 developing countries examined in this study indicates that the career aspirations of young people have little in common with current and projected labour demand, and that several job characteristics that young people value and that raise their satisfaction at work are pretty rare in many of these countries. Matching youth career aspirations and facets of job satisfaction with the reality of labour markets can play an essential role in youth well-being and social cohesion at large. In contrast, there is good reason to believe that a large employment preference gap is a significant problem. Misalignment between youth employment preferences and the availability of realistic employment prospects makes it much less likely that young people will experience smooth school-to-work transitions. A large gap might decrease motivation and productivity, fuel frustration, hamper well-being and even result in social unrest.

Reducing the youth employment preferences gap will take time, but it is possible. To address the misalignment between youth employment preferences and the availability of realistic employment opportunities, national policy makers should focus on a two-pronged strategy of: i) helping young people shape career aspirations that are realistic and that can fit with the world they will be entering, and ii) improving the quality of jobs with due regard to those job conditions that matter for young people. To be realistic, this strategy would need to be tailored to specific country contexts and recognise that the process of narrowing the gap between youth employment preferences and the reality of jobs may take time.

Notes

1. In this report, the self-employed category encompasses employers, own-account workers and members of a co-operative.

2. Typically, high-skilled occupations (ISCO 1-3) require at least some tertiary education (corresponding to the International Standard Classification of Education, ISCED, levels 3 and 4); medium-skilled occupations (ISCO 4-8) require at least some general or technical secondary certificate (ISCED 2); and low-skilled occupations (ISCO 9) require at least completion of primary school (ISCED 1).

References

AfDB/OECD/UNDP/UNECA (2012), *African Economic Outlook 2012: Promoting Youth Employment*, OECD Publishing, Paris, http://dx.doi.org/10.1787/aeo-2012-en.

Angner, E. (2012), "Subjective well-being: When, and why, it matters", *Working Paper*, University of Stockholm, https://papers.ssrn.com/sol3/papers.cfm?abstract_id=2157140.

Hyder, A. (2007), "Preference for public sector jobs and wait unemployment: a micro data analysis", *PIDE Working Papers*, Vol. 2007/20, Pakistan Institute of Development Economics, Islamabad, https://ideas.repec.org/p/pid/wpaper/200720.html.

ILO (2016), "Employment by Occupation – ILO Modelled Estimates, Nov. 2016", *ILOSTAT* (database), www.ilo.org/ilostat/faces/oracle/webcenter/portalapp/pagehierarchy/Page3.jspx?MBI_ID=12&_afrLoop=391571732018033&_afrWindowMode=0&_afrWindowId=m405vwhhl_1#!%40%40%3F_afrWindowId%3Dm405vwhhl_1%26_afrLoop%3D391571732018033%26MBI_ID%3D12%26_afrWindowMode%3D0%26_adf.ctrl-state%3Dm405vwhhl_33.

ILO (2015), *School-to-Work Transition Surveys*, International Labour Organization, Geneva, www.ilo.org/employment/areas/youth-employment/work-for-youth/WCMS_191853/lang--en/index.htm.

Mengistae, T. (1999), Wage rates and job queues: Does the public sector overpay in Ethiopia? *World Bank Policy Research Working Paper*, No. 2105, World Bank, https://papers.ssrn.com/sol3/papers.cfm?abstract_id=604989.

Mann, A., D. Massey and P. Glover (2013), "Nothing in common: The career aspirations of young Britons mapped against projected labour market demand (2010-2020)", *Occasional Taskforce Research Paper*, No. 2, Education and Employers, London, www.educationandemployers.org/research/nothing-in-common-the-career-aspirations-of-young-britons-mapped-against-projected-labour-market-demand-2010-2020-march-2013/.

Annex 3.A1. Aspirations and predicted distribution of activities

Figure 3.A1.1. Predicted distribution of activities for workers in 2021 (ILO prediction) and aspirations of students across level of qualification of occupations in developing countries (%)

Panel A. High skilled occupations (ISCO 1-3)

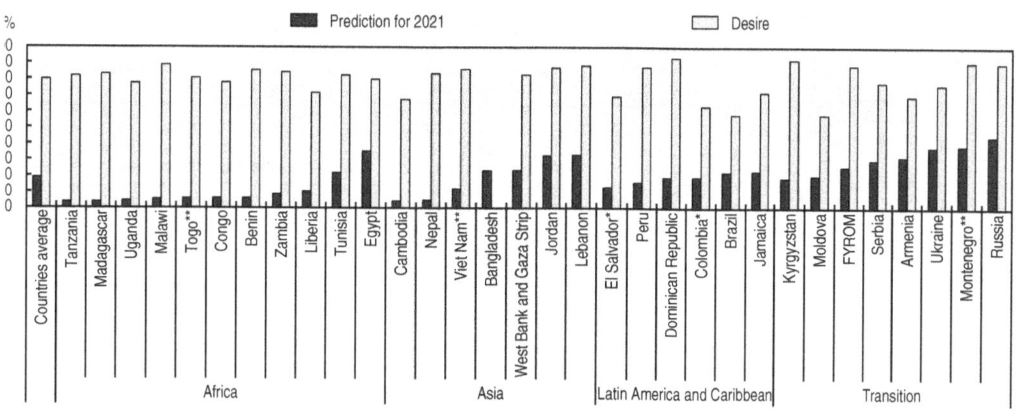

Panel B. Medium skilled occupations (ISCO 4-8)

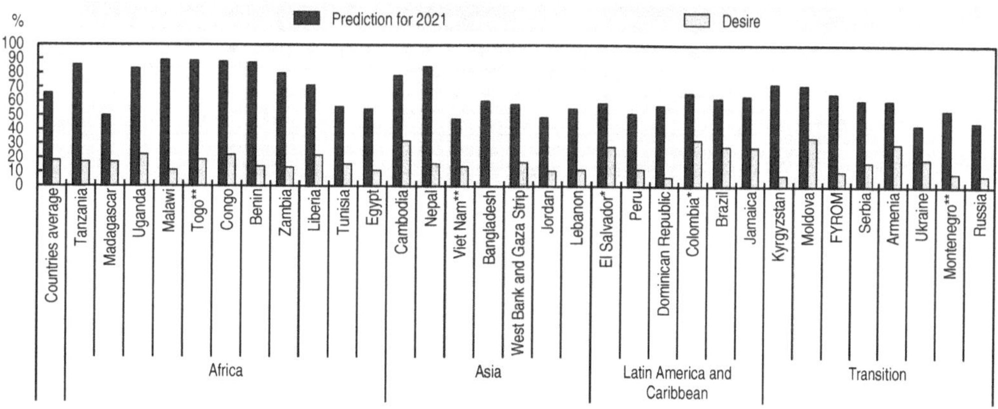

Panel C. Low skilled occupations (ISCO 9)

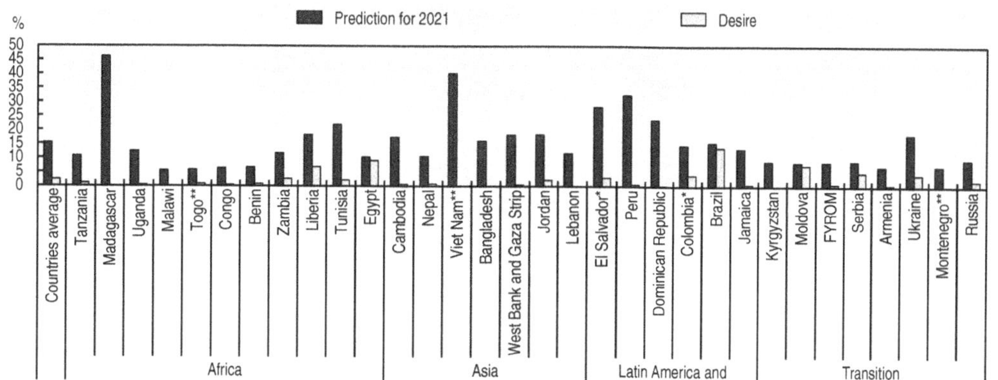

Note: Countries are sorted by the difference between the share of young students who say they want to work in a high-skilled (Panel A), medium-skilled (Panel B) or low-skilled (Panel C) occupation and the proportion of these categories for the whole working population as per the ILO's prediction for 2021. FYROM corresponds to Former Yugoslav Republic of Macedonia.

* Data for Colombia and El Salvador refer to the urban population only.

** Estimations for Montenegro, Togo and Viet Nam do not account for sampling weights as they are missing in the data.

Source: Own calculations based on School-to-Work Transition Surveys 2012-2015, and ILOSTAT (2016), "Employment by occupation – ILO modelled estimates," Nov. 2016.

Annex 3.A2. Comparison of normative and subjective skills mismatch measures

Figure 3.A1.2. **Distribution across normative skills mismatch categories of young workers who consider themselves adequately trained**

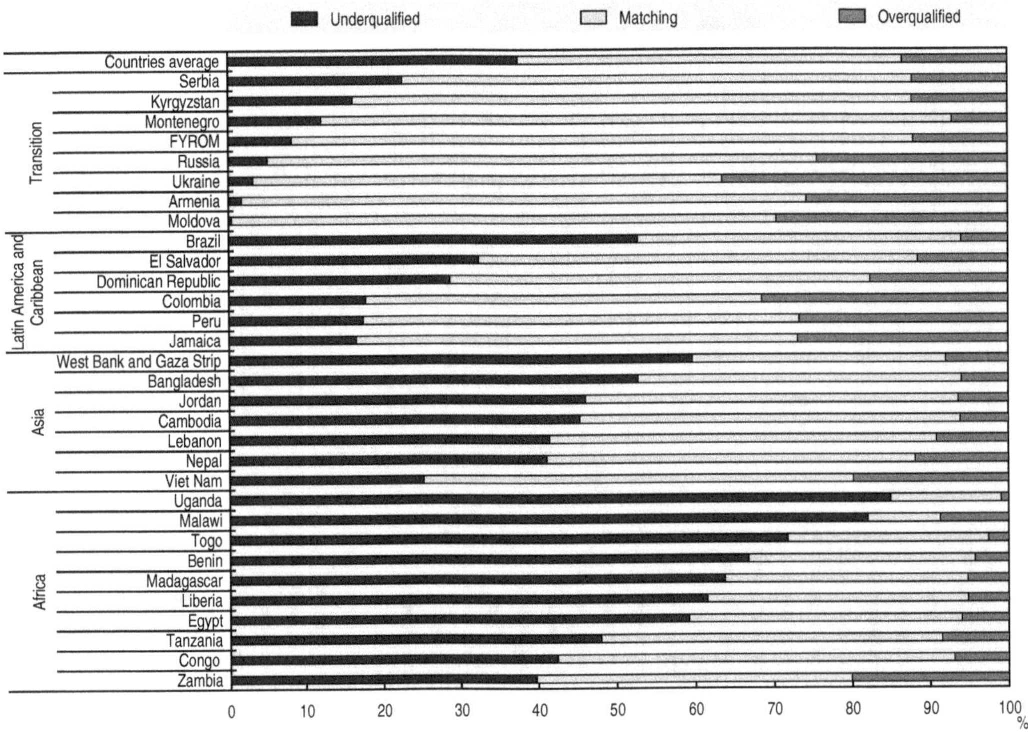

Note: Countries are sorted by the proportion of workers who consider themselves as adequately trained, but who are underqualified according to the normative measures within each group. The normative mismatch measure is based on a mapping of ISCO-08 major groups to ISCED skills levels as follows. An individual working in a high-skilled occupation (ISCO 1-3) should have completed at least some tertiary education, an individual working in a medium-skilled occupation (ISCO 4-8) should have completed (general or vocational) secondary education and an individual working in a low-skilled occupation (ISCO 9) should have completed at least primary education. These individuals are considered as adequately qualified and, if this is not the case, they enter into the over- or underqualified category. Data from Tunisia are missing.

* Data for Colombia and El Salvador refer to the urban population only. FYROM corresponds to Former Yugoslav Republic of Macedonia.

** Estimations for Montenegro, Togo and Viet Nam do not account for sampling weights as they are missing in the data.

Source: Authors' calculation, School-to-Work Transition Surveys (SWTS) 2012-2016, ILO.

ORGANISATION FOR ECONOMIC CO-OPERATION AND DEVELOPMENT

The OECD is a unique forum where governments work together to address the economic, social and environmental challenges of globalisation. The OECD is also at the forefront of efforts to understand and to help governments respond to new developments and concerns, such as corporate governance, the information economy and the challenges of an ageing population. The Organisation provides a setting where governments can compare policy experiences, seek answers to common problems, identify good practice and work to co-ordinate domestic and international policies.

The OECD member countries are: Australia, Austria, Belgium, Canada, Chile, the Czech Republic, Denmark, Estonia, Finland, France, Germany, Greece, Hungary, Iceland, Ireland, Israel, Italy, Japan, Korea, Latvia, Luxembourg, Mexico, the Netherlands, New Zealand, Norway, Poland, Portugal, the Slovak Republic, Slovenia, Spain, Sweden, Switzerland, Turkey, the United Kingdom and the United States. The European Union takes part in the work of the OECD.

OECD Publishing disseminates widely the results of the Organisation's statistics gathering and research on economic, social and environmental issues, as well as the conventions, guidelines and standards agreed by its members.

OECD DEVELOPMENT CENTRE

The OECD Development Centre was established in 1962 as an independent platform for knowledge sharing and policy dialogue between OECD member countries and developing economies, allowing these countries to interact on an equal footing. Today, 27 OECD countries and 25 non-OECD countries are members of the Centre. The Centre draws attention to emerging systemic issues likely to have an impact on global development and more specific development challenges faced by today's developing and emerging economies. It uses evidence-based analysis and strategic partnerships to help countries formulate innovative policy solutions to the global challenges of development.

For more information on the Centre and its members, please see *www.oecd.org/dev*.

OECD PUBLISHING, 2, rue André-Pascal, 75775 PARIS CEDEX 16
(41 2017 23 1 P) ISBN 978-92-64-28565-1 – 2017